Poe

Donne

Poetic Lives:
Donne

Nicholas Robins

Poetic Lives
Published by Hesperus Press Limited
19 Bulstrode Street, London w1u 2jn
www.hesperuspress.com

First published by Hesperus Press Limited, 2011

Designed and typeset by Fraser Muggeridge studio
Printed and bound by CPI Group (UK) Ltd, Croydon cr0 4yy

isbn: 978-1-84391-303-0

Contents

The poems have been taken from Herbert Grierson's 1929 edition of Donne's poetry, which preserves the spelling and some of the idiosyncrasies of the early editions. Where the titles of poems are cited within the text, however, they have been modernized.

Editions of Donne's poetry published after Grierson's have given a different order and numbering to the elegies and sonnets. These differences are highlighted within the text.

Certain impressions of the Roman religion:
Early Years

John Donne was born into a Roman Catholic family some time between 24th January and 19th June 1572 in Bread Street, in a moderately affluent district of the City of London. His father, also John, was a merchant, citizen and ironmonger and the family lived in premises owned by the Ironmongers Company, next door to William Harrison, the keeper of the Mitre Tavern, a local watering hole famous for its writers and intellectuals.

It was a prosperous household. John Donne senior was an important member of the company, promoted to warden in 1574 and given the honour, amongst others, of overseeing the decoration of the barge in which the new Lord Mayor was rowed from London to Westminster. In the early part of his career, he had been apprenticed to a successful Ironmonger and Catholic sympathiser and had subsequently risen steadily and quietly through his profession, keeping his Catholic sympathies sufficiently discreet. He also claimed gentlemanly birth. According to Isaak Walton, Donne's first biographer, the Donnes were 'masculinely and lineally descended from a very ancient family in Wales'. Donne's earliest portrait (and his monument) shows in the background the arms of the Dwns of Kidwelly in Carmathernshire, a family that drew its lineage back to the King of Dyvet, 'one of four that bare golden swords before King Arthyr at his coronation'. Less remote members of the Dwn family had successively fought with Owen Glendower against Henry IV and supported the House of York during the Wars of the Roses. What Donne did not – or did not care to – know was that the last Dwn died without male issue in 1551 and the family was already extinct before Donne was born.

The ancestry Donne later claimed through his father may have been without foundation, but his efforts to establish such a pedigree suggest something of the importance he laid upon a distinguished family and the position he sought in society. Fortunately, there was no lack of distinction on his mother's side. She was the youngest daughter of John Heywood, a musician, writer of plays or 'interludes' and a poet of great 'wit and invention'. The Catholic Heywoods had suffered for their faith. Her father, unable to accept the religious settlement under Elizabeth, had fled England in 1564, soon after his daughter's marriage to Donne's father. Ten years later, his brother Thomas, a former monk who may have conducted Donne's secret christening, was executed for saying mass. Elizabeth Donne's mother was a daughter of another literary gent, John Rastell, a printer, writer and the author of *Interlude of the Four Elements*. But most importantly, her mother's uncle had been Sir Thomas More. So on one side of his mother's family Donne could claim as a grandfather a distinguished musician and man of letters; on the other, a great, great uncle who had been Lord Chancellor of England, the author of *Utopia* and a Roman Catholic martyr.

At least eight direct descendants of More among Donne's contemporaries were members of Roman Catholic religious orders. Donne's uncles had both given up promising careers in England in order, eventually, to join the Jesuits: Ellis, a fellow of All Souls College, Oxford; and Jasper, a former page to Queen Elizabeth, a fellow of Merton College and, later, of All Souls. As a writer, Jasper is still remembered for his distinguished translations of Seneca's plays into English – the inspiration for the revenge tragedies of, amongst others, Kyd, Marlowe and the young Shakespeare. In 1562, a year after their publication, he left England for Rome to take his Jesuit vows.

It was a group bound together by a fierce fidelity to the old faith, the bitterness, perhaps, of common exile and a kinship to and reverence for Sir Thomas More. Donne's two uncles had even, it was reported in a biography of More, inherited one of the martyr's teeth and, 'either of them being desirous to have it to himself, it suddenly, to the admiration of both, parted in two.' As an adult and an intellectual, Donne would reject the cult of relics as irrelevant to true religion, but as a poet, he would prize those relics, together with many other aspects of the Roman Catholic heritage, as part of the fabric of his imagination.

The Relique

When my grave is broke up againe
Some second ghest to entertaine,
(For graves have learn'd that woman-head
To be to more then one a Bed)
And he that digs it, spies
A bracelet of bright haire about the bone
Will he not let'us alone,
And thinke that there a loving couple lies,
Who thought that this device might be some way
To make their soules, at the last busie day,
Meet at this grave, and make a little stay?

If this fall in a time, or land,
Where mis-devotion doth command,
Then, he that digges us up, will bring
Us, to the Bishop, and the King,
To make us Reliques; then
Thou shalt be a Mary Magdalen, and I
A something else thereby;

All women shall adore us, and some men;
And since at such time, miracles are sought,
I would have that age by this paper taught
What miracles wee harmelesse lovers wrought.

First, we lov'd well and faithfully,
Yet knew not what wee lov'd, nor why,
Difference of sex no more wee knew,
Then our Guardian Angells doe;
    Comming and going, wee
Perchance might kisse, but not between those meales;
    Our hands ne'r toucht the seales,
Which nature, injur'd by late law, sets free:
These miracles wee did; but now alas,
All measure, and all language, I should passe,
Should I tell what a miracle shee was.

This was the family of Donne's mother and helps to explain why she remained a devout Catholic for the rest of her life – and one in the circle of major Jesuits determined to convert England back to the old religion. Donne himself was not ignorant of his pedigree, describing himself in *Pseudo-martyr* (1610) as:

being derived of such stock and race, as, I believe, no family, (which is not of far larger extent, and greater branches,) hath endured and suffered more in their persons and fortunes, for obeying the Teachers of Roman Doctrine, then [than] it hath done.

If a line in Donne's *Devotions* (1624) is to be taken at face value his parents took a close interest in the upbringing of their children: 'My parents would not give me over to a Servant's correction.' But theirs was not a long marriage. In 1576, John Donne senior died, leaving a wife pregnant with their seventh child and an estate of some £3,500 – the equivalent of about £450,000 today, using the Retail Prices Index. He was in his early forties and his son John was then four years old.

Six months later, in July 1576, Elizabeth Donne married again, this time to John Syminges, a doctor trained at Oxford and Bologna who had several times been President of the Royal College of Physicians. Syminges was in his mid-fifties, a widower with three children and the owner of two manors in Monmouthshire. He moved his new family to Le Priors House, a good-sized property on Trinity Lane, near Cheapside, containing a parcel of land, two other houses and a garden. Not long afterwards, probably in 1577, Donne's sister Elizabeth died. The family was still living there in 1581 when, on 25th November, Mary and Katherine, Donne's two youngest siblings, were buried in the parish of Trinity the Less. This left only Anne (an elder sister), John and his younger brother Henry. Two years later, the family had moved again, this time to Bartholomew's Close in the parish of St Bartholomew the Less, an address near the hospital that would have been convenient to Syminges.

Donne's formative years, then, were spent in a medical family, with a stepfather who, in view of his wife's faith and Donne's own education, was almost certainly a discreet Roman Catholic (it was not impossible to be a successful physician while following the old faith). Donne was educated privately. An Anglican schooling at, say, Winchester, where his Oxford friend Henry Wotton went, would have been out of the question. Unquestionably he was taught by a Roman Catholic – quite possibly a seminary priest – to whom he presumably owed the early facility in Latin and French with which Walton credits him. When, following his conversion to the Church of England, he came to reflect in *Pseudo-Martyr* on the quality of his early instruction, he testified to the ideological hold his first teachers had over him:

I had a longer work to do than many other men; for I was first to blot out, certain impressions of the Roman religion, and to wrestle both against the examples and against the reasons, by which some hold was taken; and some anticipations early laid upon my conscience, both by persons who by nature had a power and superiority over my will, and others who by their learning and good life, seemed to me justly to claim an interest for the guiding, and rectifying of mine understanding in these matters.

He did not receive a Jesuit education, but he certainly came under the influence of Jesuits as a child. Jasper Heywood, his uncle, came over to England in secret as head of the Jesuit mission in 1581, when Donne was nine. It is reasonable to suppose that he made contact with his sister's family, and possibly stayed with them in the house at Trinity Lane. If so, he put his hosts in very considerable danger. Unrepentant recusants could lose their property and their homes and even be put to the sword. For the Jesuit, being caught on English soil could mean death by being hanged, drawn and quartered. It came very near this for Jasper himself when, in November 1583 (Donne being then eleven), his ship, unable to make harbour in bad weather off the French coast, was forced back to England. Jasper's identity came to light and he was promptly 'indicted of high treason for conspiring at Rheims and Rome' and thrown in the Clink prison in Southwark. He escaped execution (perhaps the Queen had in mind the service he had borne her as a page) but was kept in the Tower for a year. He was allowed visitors, and Donne's allusion much later in his life to 'a consultation of Jesuits in the Tower, in the late Queen's time' suggests that he accompanied his mother on her visits to see him.

An exclusive education in the old faith; a sense of distinguished Catholic lineage; the secretive manifestations of his uncle Jasper intent on engineering a national re-conversion to the old religion; parental whisperings and an atmosphere of intrigue: it all adds up to a sense of being set apart from others, both spiritually and intellectually. The comparison with a childhood spent among, say, a family of secret liberal intellectuals in 1930s Russia doesn't seem too fanciful.

Rather born, than made wise by study: Oxford, Cambridge and Gap Years

Donne and his brother Henry entered Oxford University on 23rd October 1584, where their ages were given as eleven and ten – a year younger than they were in each case. They were certainly young, but there are plenty of examples of others who entered the university at much the same age. The chief reason for this was that they were Roman Catholics. In 1570, the Pope had excommunicated Queen Elizabeth, declared her reign illegitimate and given moral authority to anyone who sought to disobey or even assassinate her. Any student still attending the university over the age of sixteen was therefore required to swear an oath acknowledging the supremacy of the monarch in all matters of religion and to the authority of the Thirty-Nine Articles of the Church of England. To a Roman Catholic such a requirement would have been anathema, so it was imperative to start young.

Catholicism probably also determined their choice of college – or rather, hall. Hart Hall, in common with the other halls at Oxford, was less strict than any of the colleges. It had no chapel, was presided over by Philip Rondell, said by the historian of Oxford Anthony Wood to have been a Papist 'in his heart', and had earned a reputation for having educated some prominent Catholics (two of whom had been executed for treason in recent years). It was perhaps a serious-minded, slightly isolated corner of the University. But Donne was not lonely. An aunt kept the Blue Boar Inn on St Aldate's in Oxford, and may have been charged with keeping an eye on the brothers. And Donne joined a group of talented and precocious undergraduates, many of them marked for distinction in later life. Of these, the best known, and the most long-lasting of his Oxford friendships, was Henry Wotton, later Ambassador to Venice. According to Walton, in this circle and in the University as a whole, Donne was recognised for his exceptional ability, one 'rather born, than made wise by study'.

Notwithstanding Donne's academic prestige, his family can have had no intention that he should take a degree at the end of a fourth year, which would have required that he swear the Oath of Allegiance. It was far from unusual to leave the University without a degree, although for a student of Donne's abilities, it may have been galling for his brilliance to go formally unacknowledged. Instead, he was transferred to Cambridge, where religious enforcement was at the discretion of the colleges and where in any case the University did not require students to swear the Oath. There is no formal record of his matriculation at Cambridge (the University records, unlike Oxford's, are incomplete) or of his membership of any college, but it is likely that he lodged at one of the ancient hostels in the town or perhaps with a sympathetic tutor. He did not squander his time, but was, according to Walton, 'a most laborious student, often changing his studies', which may suggest that in addition to following the curriculum he also embarked on a self-imposed course of independent study.

What kind of curriculum did Donne follow? His main subjects would have been logic and rhetoric. The ultimate end of the undergraduate course (and the basis upon which degrees were awarded) was to demonstrate some ability in disputation. His skill in dialectic is displayed in the 'Paradoxes and Problems', which also convey some flavour of the clever, impatient undergraduate. But open a volume of Donne's sermons at any page and his formal training in rhetoric is immediately evident – as it is also in 'The Flea', which was probably written some years later than his time at Lincoln's Inn.

The Flea

Marke but this flea, and marke in this,
How little that which thou deny'st me is;
It sucked me first, and now sucks thee,
And in this flea, our two bloods mingled bee;
Thou know'st that this cannot be said
A sinne, nor shame, nor losse of maidenhead,
  Yet this enjoyes before it wooe,
  And pamper'd swells with one blood made of two,
  And this, alas, is more than wee would doe.

Oh stay, three lives in one flea spare,
Where wee almost, yea more than maryed are,
This flea is you and I, and this
Our mariage bed, and mariage temple is;
Though parents grudge, and you, w'are met,
And cloystered in these living walls of jet.
  Though use make you apt to kill mee,
  Let not to this, selfe murder added bee,
  And sacrilege, three sinnes in killing three.

Cruell and sodaine, hast thou since
Purpled thy naile, in blood of innocence?
Wherein could this flea guilty bee,
Except in that drop which it suckt from thee?
Yet thou triumph'st, and saist that thou
Find'st not thyselfe, nor mee the weaker now;
  'Tis true, then learne how false, feares be;
  Just so much honor, when thou yeeld'st to mee,
  Will wast, as this flea's death tooke life from thee.

He was an early riser ('his bed', as Walton wrote, 'was not able to detain him beyond the hour of four in the morning'), and a vigorous and greedy reader. The theory of medicine; French and Italian literature; Aristotelian philosophy; civil and canon (or church) law and all that touched upon the theological controversies of the day. In addition, Donne would have discovered in Cambridge a growing literary prestige. Edmund Spenser had studied at Pembroke College not very long before; Robert Greene had studied at St John's; Marlowe had left Corpus Christi only in the last couple of years; Thomas Nashe was still at the University.

Back home, his sister Anne was married to Avery Copley, a barrister at Lincoln's Inn in 1585. Donne's stepfather died in 1588, perhaps unexpectedly (he died intestate) and was buried in the church of St Bartholomew the Less on 15th July. The administration of his estate passed to Donne's mother, and soon afterwards she took her third husband, Richard Rainsford, a 'gentleman of Southwark'. She left the house in St Bartholomew Close and moved south of the river, to the parish of St Saviours in Southwark, where her recusancy earned her an official rebuke in September 1589 for not attending communion.

At this time a hiatus appears in Donne's life, which lasts from the summer of 1589 until the spring of 1591. What seems likely – or at least possible – is that Donne undertook a continental journey that Walton ascribes (wrongly) to some eight or nine years later. Walton maintains that he spent 'some years' in Italy, and then Spain, the Spanish trip allegedly undertaken in disappointment because he had 'designed for travelling to the Holy Land, and for viewing Jerusalem and the Sepulchre of our Saviour'. For an Englishman to travel to Spain at any time between 1587 and 1604, when the two countries were at war, was not a soft alternative to Jerusalem, but if Walton is right (even if he is wrong about the dates) it may be that Donne's adherence to the old faith and his family's contacts with Jesuits active in England opened doors that would have been shut to Protestants.

There remains one alluring suggestion – it cannot be called evidence – in support of this theory. In the earliest portrait of

Donne, dated 1591, possibly by Nicholas Hilliard but known only from an engraving, there appears above the elegantly dressed youth, his locks tumbling over his collar, and his hand grasping a sword (with rather awkward determination), a motto in Spanish: *'Antes Muerto Que Mudado'*, or 'Sooner Dead than Changed'. The image complements Walton's admiring description of the young Donne:

> He was of Stature moderately tall, of a straight and equally proportioned body, to which all his words and actions gave an unexpressible addition of comeliness. The melancholy and pleasant humour, were in him so contempered, that each gave advantage to the other, and made his company one of the delights of mankind.

An hydroptique immoderate desire of humane learning and languages: Lincoln's Inn

The portrait of 1591 shows Donne at around the time he embarked on his three-year study of the law. After a minimum preparatory year at Thavies Inn, one of the Inns of Chancery in Holborn, where he learned the basics of common law, Donne entered the much grander Lincoln's Inn in 1592. In doing so he was following family tradition, for generations of his mother's side of his family, had preceded him, including Sir Thomas More, in his time a Lord Chancellor. He was never called to the Bar, but Donne's years here were of enormous importance to him. Much of his early poetry was written at Lincoln's Inn and it was in these years that his poetic voice first distinguished itself. The language and mental attitude of the law stayed with him throughout his life, leaving its impression on not just the Satires he wrote while a student at the Inn, but also the *Songs and Sonnets* and the later *Holy Sonnets*.

He also formed associations at the Inn that were to last for much of his life, including some – such as Christopher Brooke or John and Thomas Egerton, sons of the Lord Keeper – that were to be of great significance in his life and career. In not practising at the Bar he was not unusual. Less than a third of the students who joined London's Inns of Court ever practised as lawyers. The Inns were, for most of the wealthy young men who attended them, finishing schools where the student might pick up a bit of legal knowledge and skill in debating, acquire some metropolitan polish and make the kind of contacts that might provide an entrée into the wider world. In many ways, with their boisterous revels, literary enthusiasms and less austere regimens, they offered an experience closer to the modern conception of a university than either Oxford or Cambridge provided in that period – particularly for students such as John and Henry Donne, whose university careers had begun so early. The Inns were also unsparingly snobbish.

Instruction was by practice and example. Students were expected to participate in bolts (a simple case argued between students) and moots, in which inner and 'utter' barristers (i.e. those who had been called to the Bar) took part. Donne seems to have acquitted himself well and, according to Walton, 'gave great testimonies of his Wit, his Learning, and of his Improvement in that profession'. He also, Walton adds, continued his close study of a range of subjects: 'His Mother and those to whose care he was committed… appointed him Tutors both in the Mathematics, and in all the other Liberal Sciences, to attend him. But with these Arts they were advised to instil into him particular principles of the Romish Church; of which those Tutors professed (though secretly) themselves to be members.'

In his letters, Donne was to reproach himself for the avidity of his reading, and for 'the worst voluptuousness, which is an hydroptique immoderate desire of humane learning and languages'. In truth, he was caught between the two cultures of the Inn: his essentially middle-class background required him to be studious and to advance in the legal profession, but he behaved like one of the gallants whose rise through society might be achieved by contacts alone. This helps to account for the tone of the Satires; their gaze is that of an outsider, with one eye fixed contemptuously on his companions, the other, more anxious, on any opportunities for patronage and promotion. We can catch in his first Satire a glimpse of the fashionable, inquiring, impatient, contemptuous student, reluctantly dragged from his tiny 'chest' of a study packed with books – none of which seems to have any bearing on the law – and which, according to Walton, he shared with Christopher Brooke, out into the London streets:

Satyre I

Away thou fondling motley humourist,
Leave mee, and in this standing wooden chest,
Consorted with these few bookes, let me lye
In prison, and here be coffin'd, when I dye;
Here are God's conduits, grave Divines; and here
Nature's Secretary, the Philosopher;
And jolly statesmen, which teach how to tie
The sinewes of a cities mystic bodie;
Here gathering Chroniclers, and by them stand
Giddie fantastique Pöets of each land.
Shall I leave all this constant company,
And follow headlong, wild uncertaine thee?
First sweare by thy best love in earnest
(If thou which lov'st all, canst love any best)
Thou wilt not leave me in the middle street,
Though some more spruce companion thou dost meet,
Not though a Captaine do come in thy way
Bright parcell gilt, with forty dead mens pay,
Nor though brisk perfum'd piert Courtier
Deigne with a nod, thy courtesie to answer.
Nor come a velvet Justice with a long
Great traine of blew coats, twelve or fourteen strong,
Wilt thou grin or fawne on him, or prepare
A speech to Court his beauteous sonne and heire!
For better or worse take mee, or leave mee:
To take, and leave mee is adultery.
Oh monstrous, superstitious puritan,
Of refin'd manners, yet ceremoniall man,

That when thou meet'st one, with enquiring eyes
Dost search, and like a needy broker prize
The silke, and gold he weares, and to that rate
So high or low, dost raise thy formall hat:
That wilt consort none, untill thou have knowne
What lands hee hath in hope, or of his owne,
As though all thy companions should make thee
Jointures, and marry thy deare company.
Why should'st thou (that dost not onely approve,
But in rank itchie lust, desire and love
The nakednesse and barrennesse to enjoy,
Of thy plumpe muddy whore, or prostitute boy)
Hate vertue, though shee be naked, and bare?
At birth, and death, our bodies naked are;
And till our Soules be unapparelled
Of bodies, they from blisse are banished.
Man's first blest state was naked, when by sinne
Hee lost that, yet hee was cloath'd but in beast's skin,
And in this course attire, which I now weare,
With God, and with the Muses I conferre.
But since thou like a contrite penitent,
Charitably warn'd of thy sinnes, dost repent
These vanities, and giddinesses, loe
I shut my chamber doore, and come, lets goe.
But sooner may a cheape whore, who hath beene
Worne by as many severall men in sinne,
As are black feathers, or musk-colour hose,
Name her childs right true father, 'mongst all those:
Sooner one my guesse, who shall beare away
The Infanta of London, Heire to an India;
The sooner may a gulling weather Spie
By drawing forth heavens Scheme tell certainly
What fashioned hats, or ruffs, or suits next yeare
Our subtile-witted antic youths will weare;
Than thou, when thou depart'st from mee, canst show

Whither, why, when, or with whom thou wouldst go.
But how shall I be pardon'd my offence
That thus have sinn'd against my conscience?
Now we are in the street; He first of all
Improvidently proud, creepes to the wall,
And so imprisoned, and hem'd in by mee
Sells for a little state his libertie;
Yet though he cannot skip forth now to greet
Every fine silken painted foole we meet,
He them to him with amorous smiles allures,
And grins, smacks, shrugs, and such an itch endures,
As 'prentices, or schoole-boyes which doe know
Of some gay sport abroad, yet dare not goe.
And as fidlers stop lowest, at highest sound,
So to the most brave, stoops hee nigh'st the ground.
But to a grave man, he doth move no more
Than the wise politique horse would heretofore,
Or thou O Elephant or Ape wilt doe,
When any names the King of Spaine to you.
Now leaps he upright, Joggs me, and cryes, Do you see
Yonder well-favoured youth? Which? Oh, 'tis he
That dances so divinely. Oh, said I,
Stand still, must you dance here for company?
Hee droopt, wee went, till one (which did excell
Th'Indians, in drinking his Tobacco well)
Met us; they talk'd; I whispered, let us goe
'T may be you smell him not, truly I doe;
He heares not mee, but, on the other side
A many-coloured Peacock having spiede,
Leaves him and mee; I for my lost sheep stay;
He followes, overtakes, goes on the way,
Saying, 'Him whom I left last, all repute
For his device, in handsoming a sute,
To judge of lace, pinke, panes, print, cut, and pleite,
Of all the Court, to have the best conceit;

> Our dull Comedians want him, let him goe;
> But Oh, God strengthen thee, why stoop'st thou so?'
> Why? he hath travayld; Long? No. but to me
> (Which understand none), he doth seeme to be
> Perfect French, and Italian; I replyed,
> So is the pox; He answered not, but spy'd
> More men of sort, of parts, and qualities;
> At last his Love he in a windowe spies,
> And like light dew exhal'd, he flings from mee
> Violently ravish'd to his lechery.
> Many were there, he could command no more;
> He quarrell'd, fought, bled; and turned out of dore
>   Directly came to mee hanging the head,
>   And constantly a while must keepe his bed.

If Donne thrived at the Inn, he did so in spite of the plague that raged in London during his time there. The dining hall was often closed and many exercises and celebrations alike were cancelled. Donne (in what must be a testament to his popularity and ability) was appointed Master of the Revels for the Christmas period in 1592, but the festivities were cancelled that year and in fact the appointment was not made until February of the following year, so this proved an honour rather than an office. In 1594, he was chosen as Steward of Christmas, an office he declined, for which he had to pay a fine of 26s. 8d.. It was an expensive penalty to keep himself out of the limelight, but in the previous year, having turned twenty-one, he had come into his inheritance, a very substantial £750. He could now afford to be extravagant.

Something of the dull Sunday flavour of these periods of plague is caught in one of Donne's verse letters, the earliest poems he wrote. It is addressed to Everard Guilpin, a student from Suffolk at Gray's Inn, heir to a house on Highgate Hill and himself a writer of satires.

To Mr E.G.

Even as lame things thirst their perfection, so
The slimy rimes bred in our vale below,
Bearing with them much of my love and hart,
Fly unto that Parnassus, where thou art.
There thou oreseest London: here I have beene
By staying in London, too much overseene.
Now pleasures dearth our City doth posses,
Our Theatres are fill'd with emptines;
As lancke and thin is every street and way
As a woman deliver'd yesterday.
Nothing whereat to laugh my spleen espyes
But bearbaitings or Law exercise.
Therefore I'le leave it, and in the Country strive
Pleasure, now fled from London, to retrive.
Do thou so too: and fill not like a Bee
Thy thighs with honey, but as plenteously
As Russian Marchants, thy selfs whole vessell load,
And then at Winter retaile it here abroad.
Blesse us with Suffolks sweets; and as that is
Thy garden, make thy hive and warehouse this

Guilpin and his fellow students constitute the first identifiable audience for Donne's poetry; the kind of society described by Donne's contemporary Michael Drayton, which 'Spoke our own verse 'twixt ourselves, if not / Other men's lines which we by chance had got.'

The reference in the poem to having been 'overseen' alludes to a dark period during Donne's life at the Inn, for it probably refers to the government officials appointed to spy on him in 1593. The reason for it was this: Henry Donne, a year behind his brother, was in that year studying at Thavies Inn. Early in May of that year, a young Catholic priest called William Harrington had been discovered in Henry's rooms by one Richard Young, an associate of Richard Topcliffe, the most notorious executioner and torturer of Elizabeth's administration. Ironically, the Inns, which were immune from the jurisdiction of the city authorities, concealed many irregularities within their walls – including Papist cells. Harrington denied at first that he was a priest, but under cross-examination Henry Donne broke down and confessed all. Harrington was tried, imprisoned at Newgate and, in February 1594, taken to Tyburn and there hanged, taken down alive, disembowelled and quartered. Henry Donne having been a mere shelterer of the accused, it is not likely that he would have suffered the like fate, but by the time of Harrington's execution it made little difference because having been taken to the Clink and thence to Newgate at the height of the plague, he was already dead.

The circumstances of his brother's death – and for all we know Harrington was invited to stay with the elder brother as well – must have reinforced to Donne the dangerous background in which he had been raised. Harrington was no Jesuit, secretly working to convert a vulnerable Protestant nation back to the old faith, but a secular priest who spoke at his trial of his hatred for any kind of 'treachery, which I always, even from my cradle, abhorred, in thought, word, or work, against my prince or country, for whose good and at whose appointment I am ready and willing to lease my life and liberty…'

It was brought home once again to Donne that he lived in a country that refused to make a distinction between the extremism of the proselytising Jesuit, and the Roman Catholic priest dedicated to serving the spiritual needs of those ordinary, loyally disposed Catholics who remained in England. And for this situation Donne came to blame not so much the English administration as the Jesuits themselves. It was their extremism, their thirst for the martyr's crown, which so alarmed the state and constrained the lives of ordinary English Catholics – and for those who were not ordinary, but, like Donne, exceptionally ambitious and intelligent, such cramps and constraints were intolerable. It made for an unappetising choice between exile abroad and persecution at home. If he retained his faith, then worldly success or preferment was impossible; but if he were to pursue an active public life it would mean betraying his upbringing.

This forms the background to the self-imposed programme of study in theology and canon law that Donne undertook at Lincoln's Inn. According to Walton:

> he, being then unresolv'd what Religion to adhere to... begun seriously to survey, and consider the Body of Divinity, as it was then controverted betwixt the Reformed and the Roman Church... Being to undertake this search, he believed the Cardinal Bellarmine to be the best defender of the Roman cause, and therefore betook himself to the examination of his reasons...

The Bellarmine referred to was the author of a series of lectures addressed to student priests who would have to face an intellectual torrent from Protestant apologists when they returned to the Protestant lands from which they had originally come. English Jesuits such as Southwell had studied with Bellarmine, and Donne may have been directed towards his work by the Jesuits associated with his family. He was a far from uncritical reader, though, and even submitted his commentaries on the Cardinal's writings for examination by Antony Rudd, Dean of Gloucester, who had a special interest in converting and conferring with recusants. This intellectually restless, religiously sceptical period of Donne's life, when he seems to have been dissatisfied with both Catholic and Protestant theology, is clearly reflected in his third satire. It is a search for 'true religion', and its vehemence derives from the unresolved conflict between inherited beliefs amd independent thought. In fact, as John Carey writes, 'for most of its length it is not a satire at all, but a self-lacerating record of that movement which comes in the lives of almost all thinking people, when the beliefs of youth, unquestioningly assimilated and bound up with our close personal attachments, come into conflict with the scepticism of the mature intellect.'

Satyre III

Kinde pitty chokes my spleene; brave scorn forbids
Those teares to issue which swell my eye-lids,
I must not laugh, nor weepe sinnes, and be wise,
Can railing then cure these worne maladies?
Is not our Mistresse faire Religion,
As worthy of all our Soules devotion,
As vertue was to the first blinded age?
Are not heavens joyes as valiant to asswage
Lusts, as earths honour was to them? Alas,
As wee do them in meanes, shall they surpasse
Us in the end, and shall thy fathers spirit
Meete blinde Philosophers in heaven, whose merit
Of strict life may be imputed faith, and heare
Thee, whom hee taught so easie wayes and neare
To follow, damn'd? O if thou dar'st, feare this;
This feare great courage, and high valour is.
Dar'st thou ayd mutinous Dutch, and dar'st thou lay
Thee in ships woodden Sepulchres, a prey
To leaders rage, to stormes, to shot, to dearth?
Dar'st thou dive seas, and dungeons of the earth?
Hast thou couragious fire to thaw the ice
Of frozen North discoveries? and thrise
Colder than Salamanders, like divine
Children in th'oven, fires of Spaine, and the line,
Whose countries limbecks to our bodies bee,
Canst thou for gaine beare? and must every hee
Which cryes not, Goddesse! to thy Mistresse, draw,
Or eate thy poysonous words? courage of straw!

O desperate coward, wilt thou seeme bold, and
To thy foes and his (who made thee to stand
Sentinell in his worlds garrison) thus yeeld,
And for forbidden warres, leave th'appointed field?
Know thy foes: The foule Devill (whom thou
Strivest to please,) for hate, not love, would allow
Thee faine, his whole Realme to be quit; and as
The worlds all parts wither away and passe,
So the worlds selfe, thy other lov'd foe, is
In her decrepit wayne, and thou loving this,
Dost love a withered and worne strumpet; last,
Flesh (it selfs death) and joyes which flesh can taste
Thou lovest; and thy faire goodly soule, which doth
Give this flesh power to taste joy, thou dost loathe.
Seeke true religion. O where? Mirreus
Thinking her unhous'd here, and fled from us,
Seekes her at Rome, there, because hee doth know
That shee was there a thousand yeares agoe,
He loves her ragges so, as wee here obey
The statecloth where the Prince sate yesterday.
Crantz to such brave Loves will not be enthrall'd,
But loves her onely, who at Geneva is call'd
Religion, plaine, simple, sullen, yong,
Contemptuous, yet unhansome; As among
Lecherous humors, there is one that judges
No wenches wholsome, but course country drudges.
Graius stayes still at home here, and because
Some preachers, vile ambitious bawds, and laws
Still new like fashions, bid him thinke that shee
Which dwels with us, is only perfect, hee
Imbraceth her, whom his Godfathers will
Tender to him, being tender, as Wards still
Take such wives as their Guardians offer, or
Pay valewes. Carelesse Phrygius doth abhorre
All, because all cannot be good, as one

Knowing some women whores, dares marry none.
Graccus loves all as one, and thinkes that so
As women in divers countries goe
In divers habits, yet are still one kinde,
So doth, so is Religion; and this blind-
nesse too much light breeds; but unmoved thou
Of force must one, and forc'd but one allow;
And the right; aske thy father which is shee,
Let him aske his; though truth and falshood bee
Neare twins, yet truth a little elder is;
Be busie to seeke her, beleeve me this,
Hee's not of none, nor worst, that seekes the best.
To adore, or scorne an image, or protest,
May all be bad; doubt wisely; in strange way
To stand enquiring right, is not to stray;
To sleepe, or runne wrong, is. On a huge hill,
Cragged, and steep, Truth stands, and hee that will
Reach her, about must, and about must goe;
And what the hill's suddenness resists, winne so;
Yet strive so, that before age, death's twilight,
Thy Soule rest, for none can worke in that night.
To will, implyes delay, therefore now doe:
Hard deeds, the bodies paines; hard knowledge too
The mindes indeavours reach, and mysteries
Are like the Sunne, dazzling, yet plaine to all eyes.
Keepe the truth which thou hast found; men do not stand
In so ill a case here, that God hath with his hand
Sign'd Kings blanck-charters to kill whom they hate,
Not are they Vicars, but hangmen to Fate.
Foole and wretch, wilt thou let thy Soule be tyed
To mans lawes, by which she shall not be tryed
At the last day? Will it then boot thee
To say a Philip, or a Gregory,
A Harry, or a Martin taught thee this?
Is not this excuse for mere contraries,

Equally strong? cannot both sides say so?
That thou mayest rightly obey power, her bounds know;
Those past, her nature and name is chang'd; to be
Then humble to her is idolatrie;
As streames are, Power is; those blest flowers that dwell
At the rough streames calme head, thrive and prove well,
But having left their roots, and themselves given
To the streames tyrannous rage, alas, are driven
Through mills, and rockes, and woods, and at last, almost
Consum'd in going, in the sea are lost:
So perish Soules, which more chuse mens unjust
Power from God claim'd, than God himselfe to trust.

Happily, Donne's own later accounts and Walton's hagiography only give one side to his life at this time. The other side is, if not described, then at least suggested in the poems he wrote. For his time at Lincoln's Inn is the period, not just of the Satires (or at least the earliest ones), but also of the Elegies – and of some (it's impossible to say how many) of the *Songs and Sonnets*. The Elegies dramatise a quite explicit revolt against conventional attitudes and Donne's sequestered Catholic upbringing; the secret and serious comings and goings of his early life seem to find an outlet in the sense of a life secretly and closely enjoyed and in the adoption of the posture of a cynical gallant. In the sixth elegy (numbered the fourth in Grierson's edition), for instance, the poet's insecurity and superiority are flaunted in equal measure:

Elegie IV: The Perfume

Once, and but once found in thy company,
All thy suppos'd escapes are laid on mee;
And as a thiefe at barre, is question'd there
By all the men, that have beene rob'd that yeare,

So am I, (by this traiterous meanes surpriz'd)
By thy Hydroptique father catechiz'd.
Though he had wont to search with glazed eyes,
As though he came to kill a Cockatrice,
Though he hath oft sworne, that he would remove
Thy beautys beauty, and food of our love,
Hope of his goods, if I with thee were seene,
Yet close and secret, as our souls, we'have beene.
Though thy immortal mother which doth lye
Still buried in her bed, yet will not dye,
Takes this advantage to sleep out day-light,
And watch thy entries, and returnes all night,
And, when she takes thy hand, and would seeme kind,
Doth search what rings, and armelets she can finde,
And kissing notes the colour of thy face,
And fearing lest thou'art swolne, doth thee embrace;
And to trie if thou long, doth name strange meates,
And notes thy palenesse, blushing, sighs, and sweats;
And politiquely will to thee confesse
The sins of her own youths ranke lustinesse;
Yet love these Sorceries did remove, and move
Thee to gull thine owne mother for my love.
Thy little brethren, which like Faiery Sprights
Oft skipt into our chamber, those sweet nights,
And, kist and ingled on thy fathers knee,
Were brib'd next day, to tell what they did see;
The grim eight-foot-high iron-bound serving-man,
That oft names God in oathes, and onely then,
He that to barre the first gate, doth as wide
As the great Rhodian Colossus stride,
Which, if in hell no other paines there were,
Makes me feare hell, because he must be there:
Though by thy father he were hir'd to this,
Could never witnesse any touch or kisse.
But Oh, too common ill, I brought with mee

That, which betray'd mee to mine enemie:
A loud perfume, which at my entrance cryed
Even at thy fathers nose, so were wee spied.
When, like a tyran King, that in his bed
Smelt gunpowder, the pale wretch shivered.
Had it beene some bad smell, he would have thought
That his owne feet, or breath, that smell hath wrought.
But as wee in our Ile emprisoned,
Where cattel only, and diverse dogs are bred,
The precious Vnicornes, strange monsters call,
So thought he good, strange, that had none at all.
I taught my silks, their whistling to forbeare,
Even my opprest shoes, dumb and speechlesse were,
Onely, thou bitter sweet, whom I had laid
Next mee, mee traiterously hast betraid,
And unsuspected hast invisibly
At once fled unto him, and staid with mee.
Base excrement of earth, which dost confound
Sense, from distinguishing the sicke from sound;
By thee the seely Amorous sucks his death
By drawing in a leprous harlots breath;
By thee, the greatest staine to mans estate
Falls on us, to be call'd effeminate;
Though you be much lov'd in the Princes hall,
There, things that seeme, exceed substantiall.
Gods, when yee fum'd on altars, were pleas'd well,
Because you'were burnt, not that they lik'd your smell;
You'are loathsome all, being taken simply alone,
Shall wee love ill things join'd, and hate each one?
If you were good, your good doth soone decay,
And you are rare, that takes the good away.
All my perfumes, I give most willingly
To embalm thy father's corse; What? will hee die?

According to Donne's self-styled 'old acquaintance', Sir Richard Baker, an associate of Lincoln's Inn days, Donne was 'not dissolute, but very neat; a great visitor of ladies, a great frequenter of plays, a great writer of conceited verses' – and, as it seems, a great spender of his inheritance. Most of Donne's contemporaries were better acquainted with the dandy and poet than the earnest seeker after theological truth, and in a sermon to the benchers of Lincoln's Inn many years later, he alluded to the variegated lives of the young men who studied there: 'A fair day shoots arrows of visits and comedies, and conversation, and so we go abroad: and a foul day shoots arrows of gaming or chambering [or visiting prostitutes], and wantonness, and so we stay at home.'

This may be a good moment to enquire into the relationship between Donne's real life and the life described in the poems, because while a few of the *Songs and Sonnets*, Satires and Elegies may bear some kind of autobiographical reading, by no means all of them do. This seems worth saying because Donne's biographers have often assumed that the poems constitute something resembling an oblique journal of Donne's private life. This is partly Donne's fault. There is, first of all, their terrific egotism. The impassioned 'I' that is always at the centre of things makes them look, at first glance, like such promising biographical material. This misleading impression is compounded by Donne's genius for suggesting an immediate and arresting situation in his poetry. He lies in bed next to his mistress reproving the sun; later that day, or next week, or the week before, he is in the same place, considering a flea; or he is the furtive Lothario described in 'The Perfume'. It is a gift that has led some of Donne's biographers to assume a direct correspondence between the life and the poems. Sir Edmund Gosse, Donne's great Victorian biographer, fell right into the trap: 'When Donne speaks of his personal experience, there is something so convincing in his accent, poignant and rude at once, that it is impossible not to believe it the actual accurate record of a genuine emotional event.' If Gosse had called to mind the masks Robert

Browning (an admirer of Donne) explicitly wore when he composed his dramatic monologues, he might have better understood the imaginative façade that Donne has silently interposed between his agitated self and the dramatic situations he creates. When he writes so miraculously of the parting in 'The Expiration' (see p. 53), it is impossible to establish whether the situation described was written with an actual person in mind or had a basis in a real event. Donne's own occasional disclaimers suggest that it did not. In a letter he wrote in middle age to Sir Robert Ker, he even went so far as to assert that he wrote best when he wrote untruthfully. 'You know my uttermost when it was best, and even then I did best when I had least truth for my subjects.' He would probably have agreed with the view on love poetry expressed in 1593 by his contemporary, Giles Fletcher the Elder: 'A man may write of love, and not be in love, as well as of husbandry and not go to plough: or of witches, and be none: or of holiness, and be flat profane.' The biographical value of a poem like 'The Expiration' lies more in the sensibility it reveals than in the situation it seems to describe.

The autobiographical impression was further reinforced by Donne's own attitude to his poems. Throughout his life, he never wanted to be defined by his poetry and never sought to make a profession of it. He was extremely reluctant to publish his poems and insisted that they be limited to those to whom he had entrusted manuscript copies, which has suggested to some that the *Songs and Sonnets* in particular constitute a sort of covert autobiography his friends would have recognised. In fact, the reverse could be argued: his friends would best know that the situations the poems describe are fictional. It was those who did not know Donne well who might be disturbed by the suspicion that his poetry described real events. Donne himself complained of the literal way in which his love poems were sometimes read. The libertine sometimes presented in them could (in fact, did) compromise his reputation and his professional and personal prospects. By his late twenties he was expressing concern in his letters at the extent to which manuscript copies of his poetry had circulated. It was one reason why he never willingly published his poems, spoke slightingly of them, dismissing them as 'rags', and discouraged speculation about their subjects.

The Curse

Who ever guesses, thinks, or dreames he knowes
Who is my mistris, wither by this curse;
 His only, and only his purse
May some dull heart to love dispose,
And shee yeeld then to all that are his foes;
 May he be scorn'd by one, whom all else scorne,
 Forsweare to others, what to her he'hath sworne,
 With feare of missing, shame of getting, torne:

Madnesse his sorrow, gout his cramp, may hee
Make, by but thinking, who hath made him such
 And may he feele no touch
 Of conscience, but of fame, and bee
Anguish'd, not that 'twas sinne, but that 'twas shee:
 In early and long scarcenesse may he rot,
 For land which had been his, if he had not
 Himself incestuously an heire begot:

May he dreame Treason, and beleeve, that hee
Meant to performe it, and confesse, and die,
 And no record tell why:
 His sonnes, which none of his may bee,
Inherit nothing but his infamie:
 Or may he so long Parasites have fed,
 That he would faine be theirs, whom he hath bred,
 And at last be circumcis'd for bread:

The venom of all stepdames, gamsters gall,
What Tyrans, and their subjects interwish,
  What Plants, Mynes, Beasts, Foule, Fish,
  Can contribute, all ill which all
Prophets, or Poets spake; And all which shall
 Be annex'd in schedules unto this by mee,
 Fall on that man; For if it be a shee
 Nature before hand hath out-cursed mee.

Richard Baker's allusion to the frequency of Donne's playgoing is intriguing, since his period at the Inn coincides with Shakespeare's early career. If he went to the theatre often, it seems unlikely he would have missed the chance to join his fellow gallants and see the best that was on offer: a new-minted *Richard III*, perhaps, *Love's Labour's Lost*, or *Romeo and Juliet*. The Elegies bear the stamp of Marlowe's translations of Ovid's *Amores* and there are allusions to the same writer's *Tamburlaine* in 'The Calm' (see p. 45) and (unsurprisingly, perhaps) the tormented Faustus in the much later *Holy Sonnets* (see number 3 on p. 93, with its echoes of Faustus' end) and Sermons. Could he have known any of the great names in the theatre of the time? It would not have been difficult. Interested members of the audience often hobnobbed with theatrical types backstage or in the taverns of Bankside or Shoreditch. Many years later, the great actor Edward Alleyn refers in passing to the Donne of thirty years before, which may suggest that they had come across each other in Donne's youth. If so, perhaps he also came across Marlowe, the creator of Alleyn's greatest roles, or Alleyn's younger rival at the Chamberlain's Men, Richard Burbage; and if Burbage, then Shakespeare. There are very occasional suggestions of Shakespeare in Donne's poetry (consider the allusions to the mistress as page in 'On his Mistress' below), but otherwise he seems not to have made a distinctive literary impression. Nevertheless, although Donne derided the notion of writing 'labour'd scenes' for the theatre, his relation with the speakers of his poems does resemble that between a playwright and his characters and in their frequent suggestion of the soliloquy and their arresting, even vehement mode of address, they seem to bear the impression of theatrical experience.

Elegie XVI: On his Mistris

By our first strange and fatall interview,
By all desires which thereof did ensue,
By our long starving hopes, by that remorse
Which my words masculine perswasive force
Begot in thee, and by the memory
Of hurts, which spies and rivals threatned me,
I calmly beg: But by thy fathers wrath,
By all paines, which want and divorcement hath,
I conjure thee, and all the oathes which I
And thou have sworne to seale joynt constancy,
Here I unsweare, and overswear them thus,
Thou shalt not love by wayes so dangerous.
Temper, ô faire Love, loves impetuous rage,
Be my true Mistris still, not my faign'd Page;
I'll goe, and, by thy kinde leave, leave behinde
Thee, onely worthy to nurse in my minde
Thirst to come backe; ô if thou die before,
My soule from other lands to thee shall soare.
Thy (else Almighty) beautie cannot move
Rage from the Seas, nor thy love teach them love,
Nor tame wilde Boreas harshnesse; Thou hast reade
How roughly hee in peeces shivered
Faire Orithea, whom he swore he lov'd.
Fall ill or good, 'tis madnesse to have prov'd
Dangers unurg'd; Feed on this flattery,
That absent Lovers one in th'other be.

Dissemble nothing, not a boy, nor change
Thy bodies habite, nor mindes; bee not strange
To thy selfe onely; All will spie in thy face
A blushing womanly discovering grace;
Richly cloath'd Apes, are call'd Apes, and as soone
Ecclips'd as bright we call the Moone the Moone.
Men of France, changeable Camelions,
Spittles of diseases, shops of fashions,
Loves fuellers, and the rightest company
Of Players, which upon the worlds stage be,
Will quickly know thee, and no lesse, alas!
Th'indifferent Italian, as we passe
His warme land, well content to thinke thee Page,
Will hunt thee with such lust, and hideous rage,
As Lots faire guests were vext. But none of these
Nor spungy hydroptique Dutch shall thee displease,
If thou stay here. O stay here, for, for thee
England is onely a worthy Gallerie,
To walke in expectation, till from thence
Our greatest King call thee to his presence.
When I am gone, dreame me some happinesse,
Nor let thy lookes our long hid love confesse,
Nor praise, nor dispraise me, nor blesse nor curse
Openly loves force, nor in bed fright thy Nurse
With midnights startings, crying out, oh, oh
Nurse, oh my love is slaine, I saw him goe
O'r the white Alpes alone; I saw him I,
Assail'd, fight, taken, stabb'd, bleed, fall, and die.
Augure me better chance, except dread jove
Thinke it enough for me to'have had thy love.

England to whom we owe, what we be, and have: The Volunteer

At the beginning of 1596, preparations were made in England for an expedition against Spain, the largest since the one that had followed the Armada some eight years before. Its commander-in-chief was the Earl of Essex, the country's most flamboyant champion of Protestantism, and Henry Wotton, Donne's companion from Oxford days, was now one of the Earl's secretaries. Perhaps it was Wotton who gave his friend an entrée, for it was to Essex that Donne presented himself, and was accepted, for voluntary service in early 1596. For two years, John Donne was in military service.

Taking up arms for Protestant England against Catholic Spain was not the act of a devout Roman Catholic. Had he by this time converted to the Church of England? It is impossible to say, and it is in any case probably more accurate to think of his conversion as a rather drawn-out process rather than an event. What is undeniable is that the threatening shadow of Spain intensified distrust in England towards its Roman Catholic community. Signing himself up to an expeditionary fleet was a way of confirming to himself and to any prospective employers that his sympathies (as he suggests in 'The Storm') were with Protestant England rather than Papist Spain. He was also, like most of his contemporaries, won over by Essex's charm and swashbuckling panache. In later life he habitually referred to him as 'Our Earl'.

After some delays, Essex's fleet set sail on 3rd June. By 18th June it had reached Cadiz and three days later the English were cannonading the port and the three great warships that defended the inner harbour, in particular the *San Felipe*. It was almost certainly this unfortunate ship that Donne had in mind when he wrote this pitiless epigram:

A Burnt Ship

Out of a fired ship, which, by no way
But drowning, could be rescued from the flame,
Some men leap'd forth, and ever as they came
Neere the foes ships, did by their shot decay;
So all were lost, which in the ship were found,
   They in the sea being burnt, they in the burnt ship drowned.

Cadiz was stormed and taken in the same afternoon. Donne seems to have been something of a bystander in the campaign and never managed to get into the thick of things. For several days following, looting took place and the fleet set forth again on 4th July, leaving the city burning behind it. A few days later it stopped to sack and burn the deserted town of Faro. Essex took the opportunity to loot the Bishop's library and eventually brought it home and presented it to the Bodleian in Oxford. After some dithering over whether to set sail for the Azores and attack the Spanish ships returning from the West Indies, the expedition returned to Plymouth in August and Donne almost certainly returned to London.

The following year an attack on the arsenal at El Ferrol in north-west Spain was planned, again with Essex in charge, Lord Thomas Howard as vice-admiral and Walter Raleigh as rear-admiral. Again Donne volunteered, and the fleet set sail on 10th July. It quickly ran into very bad weather and Essex's and

Raleigh's squadrons returned to port; Howard's, however, made it as far as Corunna, only a short distance away, where his ships cruised for a few days, returning to Plymouth on 31st July. Donne, who complains in a letter of 'twenty days of so very, very bad weather' and that he 'had seen the land of promise Spain' was clearly part of Howard's squadron. He immortalised the storm that wrecked the venture in one of a pair of great expeditionary poems that shows his gift for vivid picture-making.

THE STORME
To Mr. *Christopher Brooke*

Thou which art I, ('tis nothing to be soe)
Thou which art still thy selfe, by these shalt know
Part of our passage; And, a hand, or eye
By Hilliard drawne, is worth an history,
By a worse painter made; and (without pride)
When by thy judgement they are dignifi'd,
My lines are such; 'Tis the preheminence
Of friendship onely to'impute excellence.
England to whom we'owe, what we be, and have,
Sad that her sonnes did seek a forraine grave
(For, Fates or Fortunes drifts none can soothsay,
Honour and misery have one face and way)
From out her pregnant intrailes sigh'd a winde
Which at th'ayres middle marble roome did finde
Such strong resistance, that it selfe it threw
Downeward againe; and so when it did view
How in the port, our fleet deare time did leese,
Withering like prisoners, which lye but for fees,
Mildly it kist our sailes, and, fresh and sweet,
As to a stomack sterv'd, whose insides meete,
Meate comes, it came; and swole our sailes, when wee

So joyd, as Sara'her swelling joy'd to see.
But 'twas but so kinde, as our countrymen,
Which bring friends one dayes way, and leave them then.
Then like two mighty Kings, which dwelling farre
Asunder, meet against a third to warre,
The South and West winds join'd, and, as they blew,
Waves like a rolling trench before them threw.
Sooner than you read this line, did the gale,
Like shot, not fear'd till felt, our sailes assaile;
And what at first was call'd a gust, the same
Hath now a stormes, anon a tempests name.
Jonas, I pitty thee, and curse those men,
Who when the storm rag'd most, did wake thee then;
Sleepe is paines easiest salve, and doth fullfill
All offices of death, except to kill.
But when I wakt, I saw, that I saw not;
I, and the Sunne, which should teach mee'had forgot
East, West, Day, Night, and I could onely say,
If'the world had lasted, now it had beene day.
Thousands our noises were, yet wee'mongst all
Could none by his right name, but thunder call:
Lightning was all our light, and it rain'd more
Than if the Sunne had drunke the sea before.
Some coffin'd in their cabins lie, 'equally
Griev'd that they are not dead, and yet must dye;
And as sin-burd'ned soules from graves will creepe,
At the last day, some forth their cabbins peepe:
And tremblingly'aske what newes, and doe heare so,
Like jealous husbands, what they would not know.
Some sitting on the hatches, would seeme there,
With hideous gazing to feare away feare.
Then note they the ship's sicknesses, the Mast
Shak'd with this ague, and the Hold and Wast
With a salt dropsie clog'd, and all our tacklings
Snapping, like too-high stretched treble strings.

And from our totterd sailes, ragges drop downe so,
As from one hang'd in chaines, a yeare agoe.
Even our Ordinance plac'd for our defence,
Strive to breake loosee, and 'scape away from thence.
Pumping hath tir'd our men, and what's the gaine?
Seas into seas throwne, we suck in againe;
Hearing hath deaf'd our saylers; and if they
Knew how to heare, there's none knowes what to say.
Compar'd to these stormes, death is but a qualme,
Hell somewhat lightsome, and the'Bermuda calme.
Darknesse, lights elder brother, his birth-right
Claims o'r this world, and to heaven hath chas'd light.
All things are one, and that one none can be,
Since all formes, uniforme deformity
Doth cover, so that wee, except God say
Another Fiat, shall have no more day.
So violent, yet long these furies bee,
That though thine absence sterve me, 'I wish not thee.

A fortnight later, he was away again, setting out for Spain on 15th August. The expedition once again encountered bad weather and the fleet split in two. The planned attack on El Ferrol was abandoned and Essex, hearing a rumour that a Spanish fleet from the West Indies was making for the Azores, made a dash for the islands. But when Donne's part of the fleet, commanded by Raleigh rather than Essex, arrived in early September, it was becalmed for at least two days. Donne recorded the event in 'The Calm', his companion piece to 'The Storm', in which he also describes some of his personal motives for joining the expedition: to put an end to the extravagant living he had enjoyed at Lincoln's Inn, make up his losses with booty and to satisfy a more general restlessness and desire for action. Both poems came to be amongst the most admired in Donne's lifetime.

THE CALME

Our storme is past, and that storms tyrannous rage,
A stupid calme, but nothing it, doth swage.
The fable is inverted, and farre more
A blocke afflicts, now, than a storke before.
Stormes chafe, and soone weare out themselves, or us;
In calms, Heaven laughs to see us languish thus.
As steady'as I can wish, that my thoughts were,
Smooth as thy mistresse glasse, or what shines there,
The sea is now. And, as those Iles which wee
Seeke, when wee can move, our ships rooted bee.
As water did in stormes, now pitch runs out
As lead, when a fir'd Church becomes one spout.
And all our beauty, and our trimme, decayes,
Like courts removing, or like ended playes.
The fighting place now seamens ragges supply;
And all the tackling is a frippery.
No use of lanthornes; and in one place lay
Feathers and dust, to day and yesterday.
Earth's hollownesses, which the world's lungs are,
Have no more winde then the upper vault of aire.
We can nor lost friends, nor sought foes recover,
But meteorlike, save that wee move not, hover.
Onely the Calenture together drawes
Deare friends, which meet dead in great fishes jawes:
And on the hatches as on Altars lyes
Each one, his owne Priest, and owne Sacrifice.
Who live, that miracle do multiply
Where walkers in hot Ovens, doe not dye.
If in despite of these, wee swimme, that hath
No more refreshing, than our brimstone Bath,
But from the sea, into the ship we turne,
Like parboil'd wretches, on the coales to burne.
Like Bajazet encag'd, the shepheards scoffe,

Or like slack-sinew'd Sampson, his haire off,
Languish our ships. Now, as a Myriade
Of Ants, durst th'Emperours lov'd snake invade,
The crawling Gallies, Sea-goales, finny chips,
Might brave our Pinnaces, now bed-ridde ships.
Whether a rotten state, and hope of gaine,
Or to disuse mee from the queasie paine
Of being belov'd, and loving, or the thirst
Of honour, or faire death, our pusht mee first,
I lose my end: for here as well as I
A desperate joy may live, and a coward die.
Stagge, dogge, and all which from, or towards flies,
Is paid with life, or prey, or doing dyes.
Fate grudges us all, and doth subtly lay
A scourge, 'gainst which wee all forget to pray,
He that at sea prayes for more winde, as well
Under the poles may begge cold, heat in hell.
What are wee then? How little more alas
Is man now, than before he was! he was
Nothing; for us, wee are for nothing fit;
Chance, or our selves still disproportion it.
Wee have no power, no will, no sense; I lye,
I should not then thus feele this miserie.

Once the calm had lifted, the English ships cruised for a few days, in the end missing nearly all the Spanish West Indian fleet, which slipped safely and contemptuously into the heavily fortified harbour at Angra only a few hours after the English ships had left the island. Apart from the capture of three Spanish ships which had arrived later than the rest, the sole success of the rather futile expedition was the capture of two towns: Fayal, overrun by Raleigh (at which Donne may have been present) but deserted and bare of loot, and Villa Franca, taken by Essex. Here the adventurers rested and the Earl created some knights. On

9th October, a few days short of two months after setting out, the fleet, carrying Donne with it, left the Azores and made for home.

Some more weighty employment:
The Secretary

One of the young men knighted by Essex at Villa Franca was Donne's friend Thomas Egerton, son of the Lord Keeper of the Great Seal. It is likely that Donne's association with the young Egerton on the expedition, and earlier at Lincoln's Inn, earned him his introduction to the Lord Keeper himself, for in or around November 1597 he was engaged as one of his secretaries.

The elder Sir Thomas Egerton was a man of very considerable abilities. He had overcome a disadvantageous birth (he was illegitimate) and been forgiven his open Catholic recusancy at Oxford to become in turn Solicitor General, Attorney General and Master of the Rolls. In these capacities, he had taken a leading part in a number of important trials, including those of Edmund Campion and Mary Queen of Scots. He had been appointed Lord Keeper in 1596, an office that included presiding over the House of Lords and acting as an intermediary between Parliament and the Crown. His place on the Privy Council required him to decide on important matters of state on a daily basis. He occupied a position comparable to that of a senior cabinet minister today, and if Thomas Fuller is to be believed, he looked the part, too: 'Christendom afforded not a person which carried more gravity in his countenance and behaviour.' By attaching himself to Egerton, Donne had good reason to expect that he would, in time, enjoy a fast track to senior public office. And according to Walton, Egerton shared the same ambition for his new secretary, 'supposing and intending it to be an introduction to some more weighty employment in the state; for which, his lordship did often protest, he thought him very fit'.

The Lord Keeper's extensive royal and parliamentary duties called for Donne's secretarial assistance at Whitehall, and one of his duties was to convey messages from the various councils to wherever the Queen happened to be. He was also employed in much of the legal work that reached the Lord Keeper's desk. Egerton was determined to reform court procedure and Donne was given the responsibility of looking into the exorbitant fees charged to suitors by lawyers and court officials. His Fifth Satire reveals that he was shocked and indignant at what he discovered.

> *O age of rusty iron! Some better wit*
> *Call it some worse name, if ought equall it;*
> *The iron Age that was, when justice was sold; now*
> *Injustice is sold dearer farre. Allow*
> *All demands, fees and duties, gamsters, anon*
> *The mony which you sweat, and sweare for, is gon*
> *Into other hands: So controverted lands*
> *Scape, like Angelica, the strivers hands.*

Egerton seems to have been a good and kindly employer, enjoying the company of the staff who worked under him. He never, according to Walton, forgot that Donne 'was his friend; and to testify it, did always use him with much courtesy, appointing him a place at his own table, to which he esteemed his company and discourse to be a great ornament'. The table at which Donne found himself was at York House, the rambling old pile on London's Strand, officially the residence of the Archbishop of York but in those days leased out on a permanent basis to the Lord Keeper and his family. Here lived, in the midst of an extensive staff, Sir Thomas and his second wife, Elizabeth, the two sons from his first marriage – the younger Sir Thomas (with his wife and three little daughters) and John, a student at Lincoln's Inn. There were also, amongst others, relations of Lady Egerton, including a niece, Ann More, a girl, according to Walton, 'curiously and plentifully educated', whom her aunt was bringing up as a favour to her brother.

How soon it was after moving in to York House that Donne, now around twenty-six years old, fell in love with the fourteen-year-old Ann More (the age of Shakespeare's Juliet), and she with him, it is impossible to say. Their illicit romance, begun perhaps at the supper table at her uncle's house, may have been pursued in secret in the crowded passageways of York House or perhaps in the maze of courtyards and gardens of Whitehall Palace when Donne's business took him there. Under the watchful eye of her aunt – at least for the first year of Donne's period at York House – the opportunities to be alone together were probably few. And there could be absolutely no possibility of their relationship coming to light. The revelation would be, for Donne, professionally disastrous.

Ann was the daughter of Sir George More, a distinguished MP and man of affairs who had travelled with Sir Philip Sidney and been knighted by Elizabeth I, and who had once written a fervent, if dull, work of theology. Sir George lived in a lavish style at the family estate near Guildford, where he was given to fearful bouts of wrath. Ann was the third of five daughters and her four sisters were all destined to marry into wealthy country families. Donne, brilliant, unorthodox and, notwithstanding his good prospects, not well off, was not at all the steady kind of man Sir George had in mind for his third daughter.

What was Ann like? Unfortunately, all Donne's biographers regretfully agree that, as an individual, we know almost nothing about her. The suggestion of affection and companionship that characterises some of the *Songs and Sonnets* is sometimes attributed to the appearance of Ann in Donne's life.

The good-morrow

I wonder by my troth, what thou, and I
Did, till we lov'd? were we not wean'd till then?
But suck'd on countrey pleasures, childishly?
Or snorted we in the seaven sleepers den?
T'was so; But this, all pleasures fancies bee.
If ever any beauty I did see,
Which I desir'd, and got, t'was but a dreame of thee.

And now good morrow to our waking soules,
Which watch not one another out of feare;
For love, all love of other sights controules,
And makes one little roome, an every where.
Let sea-discoverers to new worlds have gone,
Let Maps to other, worlds on worlds have showne,
Let us possesse one world, each hath one, and is one.

My face in thine eye, thine in mine appeares,
And true plaine hearts doe in the faces rest,
Where can we finde two better hemispheares
Without sharpe North, without declining West?
What ever dyes, was not mixt equally;
If our two loves be one, or, thou and I
Love so alike, that none doe slacken, none can die.

Early in 1599, the household lost the company of the younger Sir Thomas, who had joined the Earl of Essex on his ill-fated expedition to Ireland. And in August of the same year, tragedy struck. The 25-year-old volunteer was fatally wounded in a skirmish and died at Dublin Castle. His body was brought over the water to Chester for burial. Public business kept his father in London, and he was unable to attend the solemn and magnificent funeral in the cathedral, but Donne made the journey north, and had the honour of carrying his old companion's sword in the funeral procession. His elegy 'On Sir Thomas Egerton' commemorates his friend.

Not the least of Egerton's duties in London was having to respond to the crisis caused by the Earl of Essex himself, who had returned from Ireland in defiance of the Queen's orders and forced his way into the royal presence at Nonsuch Palace. This insult cost him his position at court and he was given over to Egerton and detained at York House – which is probably where he was when Donne returned from Chester. Essex's presence cannot have brought much tranquillity to the household. As an earl, his rank demanded special treatment, and, what was worse, he fell ill. Donne now had the opportunity to see in less favourable circumstances the charismatic figure whose example had partly persuaded him and many of his friends to join the expeditions against Spain not long before. Close to, his former follower was less impressed, observing shrewdly that, 'The worst accidents of his sickness are that he conspires with it and that it is not here believed.' Meanwhile, court affairs and festivities proceeded as usual. Shakespeare's company performed plays at Greenwich and Donne, whose duties now brought him within its orbit, found the court in general 'full of jollity and revels and plays and as merry as if it were not sick'. The court no more lamented the absence of Essex and his train than had the heavenly host missed 'the angels which were cast down from heaven nor (for anything I see) likelier to return'.

In January 1600, the situation was made immeasurably worse by a further death in the family – this time of Egerton's wife. The widower was plunged into grief and unable for at least a week to meet the challenge of daily business. And from Donne's point of view there was a second blow: with no guardian to keep her in London, Ann was returned to live at Loseley, her father's estate in Surrey. They pledged themselves to each other, but they could not be sure that they would ever see each other again. Although there is no evidence that 'The Expiration' was written before 1602, it seems designed for the unhappy parting.

The Expiration

So, so, breake off this last lamenting kisse,
  Which sucks two soules, and vapors Both away,
Turne thou ghost that way, and let mee turne this,
  And let our selves benight our happiest day,
We ask'd none leave to love; nor will we owe
  Any, so cheape a death, as saying, Goe;

Goe; and if that word have not quite kil'd thee,
  Ease mee with death, by bidding mee goe too.
Oh, if it have, let my word worke on mee,
  And a just office on a murderer doe.
Except it be too late, to kill me so,
  Being double dead, going, and bidding, goe.

In the following March, Essex's health improved and (no doubt with relief all round) he was permitted to make the short journey to Essex House, where his house arrest continued. Later in the summer the Earl was given his liberty, but his office was not renewed and in the autumn the Queen refused to renew his tax grant on sweet wines, his chief source of income. In November, Egerton married again and the installation of his bride, the Countess of Derby, threw York House into disarray. Her large entourage probably left no room for Donne, who was obliged to move to premises further down the Strand, near the Savoy.

Meanwhile, impatient, resentful and desperate, Essex had surrounded himself with a coterie of faithful followers and disaffected types, and was plotting to mend his marred fortunes by force. His not very covert activities came to the notice of the Lord Keeper and other members of the Council, who summoned Essex to appear before them. Essex ignored the summons and on the morning of 18th February 1601, a party that included the Lord Keeper, the Lord Chief Justice and a group of retainers (of whom Donne is likely to have formed a part), demanded entry to Essex House. The councillors, but not the retinue, were invited in, and then, in a sudden moment of farce, were locked in the study by Essex himself, who then made for the City to raise a force against Whitehall. Here they were kept until shortly before Essex returned from his aborted coup. That night, the Earl was led from his house to prison.

Donne must have been appalled by Essex's fall, and even more by the fate of those who had supported him. Had he not found a position in Egerton's office, he might have joined the Earl's expedition to Ireland and perhaps eventually followed him to the scaffold. He was probably involved in the gathering of evidence for the trial of Essex and his co-conspirators, but he was shocked by the hypocritical lengths to which some others went to save their own skins. The youngish Francis Bacon, for instance, who had placed all hopes of preferment on Essex, turned on his old patron with forensic ruthlessness and drafted the official report of Essex's crimes. Donne's copy of the report survives, and bears an ironic inscription, '*Sinite cum Maledicere nam Dominus iussit*', from 2 Samuel 16.10: 'Let him curse even because the Lord hath bidden him.'

Donne's friend from university days, Henry Wotton, was one of those who had lost his position when Essex had lost his. The letters and verse letters that passed between them (Donne's in particular) share a deep contempt for court, public and country life alike and show signs of the fashionable Senecan stoicism of the age. The only answer was to be 'thine own home, and in thy self dwell' – a familiar idea in many of the *Songs and Sonnets*.

The Anniversarie

All Kings, and all their favorites,
    All glory of honors, beauties, wits,
The Sun it selfe, which makes times, as they passe,
Is elder by a yeare, now, then it was
When thou and I first one another saw:
All other things, to their destruction draw,
    Only our love hath no decay;
This, no to morrow hath, nor yesterday,
Running it never runs from us away,
But truly keepes his first, last, everlasting day.

    Two graves must hide thine and my coarse,
    If one might, death were no divorce.
Alas, as well as other Princes, wee,
(Who Prince enough in one another bee,)
Must leave at last in death, these eyes, and eares,
Oft fed with true oathes, and with sweet salt teares;
    But soules where nothing dwells but love
(All other thoughts being inmates) then shall prove
This, or a love increased there above,
When bodies to their graves, soules from their graves remove.

    And then wee shall be throughly blest,
    But wee no more, then all the rest;
Here upon earth, we'are Kings, and none but wee
Can be such Kings, nor of such subjects bee.
Who is so safe as wee? where none can doe
Treason to us, except one of us two.
    True and false feares let us refraine,
Let us love nobly, and live, and adde againe
Yeares and yeares unto yeares, till we attaine
To write threescore: this is the second of our raigne.

As well as keeping up old friendships, Donne also made new ones during his period in Egerton's service, including the Herbert family. His friendship with Magdalen Herbert (the mother of the poets George and Sir Edward Herbert of Cherbury) was to prove one of the most long-lived of his life, His first meeting with her, which may have taken place in Oxford, probably inspired his 15th elegy (or ninth in Grierson's edition) – although, as has often been pointed out, thirty-two, as she was then, seems very young to be described as 'autumnal'.

ELEGIE IX
The Autumnall

No Spring, nor Summer Beauty hath such grace,
*   As I have seen in one Autumnall face.*
Young Beauties force your love, and that's a Rape,
*   This doth but counsaile, yet you cannot scape.*
If t'were a shame to love, here t'were no shame,
*   Affection here takes Reverences name.*
Were her first yeares the Golden Age; that's true,
*   But now shee's gold oft tried, and ever new.*
That was her torrid and inflaming time,
*   This is her tolerable Tropique clime.*
Faire eyes, who asks more heate than comes from hence,
*   He in a fever wishes pestilence.*
Call not these wrinkles, graves; if graves they were,
*   They were Loves graves; for else he is nowhere.*
Yet lies not Love dead here, but here doth sit
*   Vowed to this trench, like an Anachorit.*
And here, till hers, which must be his death, come,
*   He doth not dig a Grave, but build a Tombe.*
Here dwells he, though he sojourne ev'ry where
*   In Progresse, yet his standing house is here.*
Here, where still Evening is; not noone, nor night;

Where no voluptuousnesse, yet all delight,
In all her words, unto all hearers fit,
You may at Revels, you at Counsaile, sit.
This is love's timber, youth his under-wood;
There he, as wine in June, enrages blood,
When then comes seasonabliest, when our tast
And appetite to other things, is past.
Xerxes strange Lydian love, the Platane tree,
Was lov'd for age, none being so large as shee,
Or else because, being yong, nature did blesse
Her youth with age's glory, Barrennesse.
If we love things long sought, Age is a thing
Which we are fifty years in compassing.
If transitory things, which soone decay,
Age must be lovelyest at the latest day.
But name not Winter-faces, whose skin's slacke;
Lanke, as an unthrifts purse; but a soules sacke;
Whose Eyes seeke light within, for all here's shade;
Whose mouthes are holes, rather worne out, then made;
Whose every tooth to a severall place is gone,
To vexe their souls at Resurrection;
Name not these living Deaths-heads unto mee,
For these, not Ancient, but Antique be.
I hate extreames; yet I had rather stay
With Tombs, then Cradles, to weare out a day.
Since such loves naturall lation is, may still
My love descend, and journey downe the hill,
Not panting after growing beauties, so,
I shall ebbe out with them, who home-ward goe.

Donne's most ambitious and, depending on your point of view, most disappointing or most underrated poem, dates from August 1601 – a work undertaken, perhaps, to occupy himself in Ann's absence. 'The Progress of the Soul' or 'Metempsychosis' is a satirical epic relating the history of a single soul in its journey up the food chain, from the apple eaten by Eve, through a bird, fishes, a whale, land mammals and eventually (in its unfinished state) to the sister and wife of Cain, taking some savage swipes at courtly and public life en route. Scholars disagree about where the soul was intended to end up had Donne finished the poem. Ben Jonson maintained it would be Calvin, but some lines in the sixth stanza make it clear that the soul's last port of call would be England:

> *For though through many streights, and lands I roame,*
> *I launch at paradise, and I saile towards home;*
> *The course I there began, shall here be staid,*
> *Sailes hoised there, struck here, and anchors laid*
>   *In Thames, which were at Tigrys, and Euphrates waide.*

And the implication of the lines that follow in the next stanza is that its ultimate lodging would be Queen Elizabeth or her first minister Robert Cecil:

> *For the great soule which here amongst us now*
> *Doth dwell, and moves that hand, and tongue, and brow,*
> *Which, as the Moone the sea, moves us; to heare*
> *Whose story, with long patience you will long;*
> *(For 'tis the crowne, and last straine of my song)*

The poem shows more clearly than in anything else he wrote Donne's interest in biology and anatomy. There are some miraculous passages, including those describing the soul's entry into a bird –

> *To an unfetterd soules quick nimble hast*
> *Are falling stars, and hearts thoughts, but slow pac'd:*
> *Thinner then burnt aire flies this soule, and she*
> *Whom foure new comming, and foure parting Suns*

Had found, and left the Mandrakes tenant, runnes
Thoughtlesse of change, when her firme destiny
Confin'd, and enjayld her, that seem'd so free,
Into a small blew shell, the which a poore
Warme bird orespread, and sat still evermore,
      Till her inclos'd child kickt, and pick'd it selfe a dore.

Outcrept a sparrow, this soules moving Inne,
On whose raw armes stiffe feathers now begin,
As childrens teeth through gummes, to breake with paine,
His flesh is jelly yet, and his bones threds,
All a new downy mantle overspreads,
A mouth he opes, which would as much containe
As his late house, and the first houre speaks plaine,
And chirps alowd for meat. Meat fit for men
His father steales for him, and so feeds then
      One, that within a moneth, will beate him from his hen.

Or this, its entry into a fish –

This cole with overblowing quench'd and dead,
The Soule from her too active organs fled
T'a brooke. A female fishes sandie Roe
With the males jelly, newly lev'ned was,
For they had intertouch'd as they did passe,
And one of those small bodies, fitted so,
This soule inform'd, and abled it to row
It selfe with finnie oares, which she did fit:
Her scales seem'd yet of parchment, and as yet
      Perchance a fish, but by no name you could call it.

Or this, the soul's transference from the 'toyful' ape who has enjoyed the society of Adam's fifth daughter, to a human being:

This Ape, though else through-vaine, in this was wise,
He reach'd at things too high, but open way
There was, and he knew not she would say nay;
His toyes prevaile not, likelier meanes he tries,
He gazeth on her face with teare-shot eyes,
And up lifts subtly with his russet pawe
Her kidskinne apron without feare or awe
  Of Nature; nature hath no gaole, though shee hath law.

First she was silly and knew not what he ment,
That vertue, by his touches, chaft and spent,
Succeeds an itchie warmth, that melts her quite;
She knew not first, nowe cares not what he doth,
And willing halfe and more, more than halfe loth,
She neither puls nor pushes, but outright
Now cries, and now repents; when Tethlemite
Her brother, entred, and a great stone threw
After the Ape, who, thus prevented, flew.
  This house thus batter'd downe, the Soule possest a new.

It is worth reiterating here that Donne's poems – even long narrative poems such as 'The Progress of the Soul' – were almost never intended for publication, but always circulated in manuscript. The only poetry he was ever persuaded to publish, *The Anniversaries*, came to be a cause of vexation and regret. Why was this? One reason was that he relished exclusivity. 'His poems,' in the words of John Stubbs, 'went into the world as handwritten letters or gifts for people he cared about or respected, not impersonal publications that just anyone could pick up from one of the bookshops clustered around the churchyard of St Paul's.' A second was that he feared for his reputation, even his liberty. Only two years before 'The Progress of the Soul', Church of England bishops had instituted a clampdown on satires, epigrams, erotic poetry and English histories. There had been a book burning at Stationers' Hall (where all unpublished manuscripts were registered for publication) and titles by Marlowe, Nashe and Marston had been thrown on the flames. Donne, ambitious for public office, had no intention of seeing his own work – and reputation – join the pyre. Donne's prose 'Paradoxes' date from this time, and in a covering letter he sent with them (probably to Wotton), his anxiety over publication or, in this case, even transcription, is evident: '[E]xcept I receive by your next letter an assurance upon the religion of your friendship that no copy shall be taken for any respect of these or any other my compositions sent to you, I shall sin against my conscience if I send you any more... to my Satires there belongs some fear, and to some Elegies, and these perhaps, shame... Therefore I am desirous to hide them, without any over-reckoning of them or their maker.'

His caution is unsurprising, for by the end of 1601 he had a lot to lose. He was at the high point of his career as a public servant. In the Parliament that sat from 27th October to 19th December his employer arranged for him to sit as the MP for Brackley in Northamptonshire (he does not seem to have contributed to debates). Although the precariousness of office lay often at the front of his mind, he could not know that his promising career was almost at an end.

It is irremediably done:
Marriage

In October 1601, when parliament assembled, Ann More returned to London with her father. Donne learned of her return and, 'twice or thrice', as he admitted later, they met secretly. Donne, still very far from Sir George's idea of a suitable match for his daughter, had no hope of achieving her father's consent to their union. What is more, Ann would soon have to return to Loseley Park and there would be no further opportunities to meet. The lovers sought a desperate solution. Some three weeks before Christmas (the exact date is unknown), in the presence of Christopher Brooke, Donne's old friend from Lincoln's Inn days, and with Brooke's ordained brother Samuel officiating, the couple were secretly married in the Anglican rite – probably, as R.C. Bald speculates, in the chapel of the Savoy, which was technically a 'liberty' and so outside the city authorities and only a few steps from Donne's lodgings. It later became a notorious venue for clandestine marriages.

Having kept their marriage secret, the couple had to choose very carefully the right moment to impart the news to Ann's father. Under any circumstances this was bound to be a ticklish task since it was axiomatic that families should be closely involved in the arrangement of marriages. The views of Walton (for whom Donne's marriage was the great blunder of his life) speak largely for the time: 'love is a flattering mischief... that carries us to commit errors with as much ease as whirlwinds remove feathers'; it was a marriage made 'without the allowance of those friends, whose approbation always was, and ever will be necessary, to make even a virtuous love become lawful'. Moreover, Ann was still a minor, her father's chattel, and Sir George was a notoriously choleric man.

Two months passed in a state of painful indecision and Donne's anxiety eventually made him ill. He did not make the announcement to Sir George in person, but through the offices of the most distinguished friend he could find. This was Henry Percy, ninth Earl of Northumberland (later known as the 'wizard earl'), who as the scion of a great Catholic family and Sir George's social superior may have been a tactless choice of emissary. The letter he carried from Donne to Ann's father anticipated the worst: 'I know this letter shall find you full of passion; but I know no passion can alter your reason and wisdom, to which I adventure to commend these particulars; that it is irremediably done; that if you incense my lord you destroy her and me; that it is easy to give us happiness, and that my endeavours and industry, if it please you to prosper them, may soon make me somewhat worthier of her.'

If he hoped that by anticipating the storm he would contain it, he was mistaken. Sir George was incensed. He went straight to the Lord Keeper's office and complained of a breach of canon law (the marriage had been made without consent and in Advent). Donne was committed to the foul and unhealthy Fleet prison and Samuel and Christopher Brooke, as accessories, were sent to the Marshalsea. By now seriously ill, Donne wrote again to Sir George, this time more abjectly, protesting that 'all my endeavours, and the whole course of my life shall be bent, to make myself worthy of your favour and her love, whose peace of conscience and quiet I know must be much wounded and violenced if your displeasure sever us.' But while the hectic raged in Sir George's blood, all pleas were unavailing. Donne was allowed to return to his lodgings (where he was confined), but Sir George pressed the Lord Keeper to sack him – which, after some hesitation and much reluctance, Egerton did.

It was only later that Sir George seems to have realised that, if the High Commissioners recognised the marriage (as, in fact, they were bound to do), it was not just Donne who would suffer by losing his position; Ann would too. By the beginning of March, his confinement lifted, and having helped to secure the enlargement of the Brookes (a profound embarrassment), Donne persuaded Sir George to ask Egerton to reinstate him, and wrote to Egerton himself, declaring that 'The sickness of which I died is, that I began in your lordship's house this love. Where I shall be buried I know not.' But it was too late. Neither his servant's plea, nor Sir George's support could prevail. Even though he parted with 'such a secretary as was fitter to serve a King than a subject' Egerton would not go back on his decision, it being, in Walton's words, 'inconsistent with his place and credit, to discharge and readmit servants at the request of passionate petitioners'.

The Canonization

For Godsake hold your tongue, and let me love,
  Or chide my palsie, or my gout,
My five grey haires, or ruin'd fortune flout,
  With wealth your state, your minde with Arts improve,
    Take you a course, get you a place,
    Observe his honour, or his grace,
Or the Kings reall, or his stamped face
  Contemplate, what you will, approve,
  So you will let me love.

Alas, alas, who's injur'd by my love?
  What merchants ships have my sighs drown'd?
Who saies my teares have overflow'd his ground?
  When did my colds a forward spring remove?
    When did the heats which my veines fill

Adde one more to the plaguie Bill?
Soldiers finde warres, and Lawyers finde out still
   Litigious men, which quarrels move,
   Though she and I do love.

Call us what you will, wee are made such by love;
   Call her one, mee another flye,
We'are Tapers too, and at our owne cost die,
   And wee in us finde the'Eagle and the Dove.
      The phoenix ridle hath more wit
      By us, we two being one, are it.
So, to one neutrall thing both sexes fit,
   Wee dye and rise the same, and prove
   Mysterious by this love.

Wee can dye by it, if not live by love,
   And if unfit for tombes and hearse
Our legend bee, it will be fit for verse;
   And if no peece of Chronicle wee prove,
      We'll build in sonnets pretty roomes;
      As well a well wrought urne becomes
The greatest ashes, as halfe-acre tombes,
   And by these hymnes, all shall approve
   Us Canoniz'd for love.

And thus invoke us; You whom reverend love
   Made one anothers hermitage;
You, to whom love was peace, that now is rage;
   Who did the whole worlds soule contract, and drove
      Into the glasses of your eyes,
      So made such mirrors, and such spies,
That they did all to you epitomize,
   Countries, Townes, Courts: Beg from above
   A patterne of your love!

And so Donne found himself, at the age of thirty, out of a job, in debt to the tune of £40 (arising from the costs of the case and of securing the release of his friends) with no prospect of material support from his father-in-law, and a young wife to care for. The best and only course open to both of them seemed to be to lie low until the scandal had blown over. With Egerton's help, they took possession of a £100 legacy left by Ann's aunt, Egerton's late wife, and accepted the invitation of Ann's cousin, Francis Wolley to stay at his country house at Pyrford, some eight miles from Guildford, and within striking distance of Loseley Park.

Here, John and Ann Donne spent the first years of their marriage in a house, according to John Evelyn, of 'timber, but commodious, and with one ample dining room, and the hall adorned with paintings of foul and huntings etc.'. 'Elegy 2' (or 19 in Grierson's edition) is usually placed some years earlier, but it is possible that it dates from their time at Pyrford.

ELEGIE XIX
Going to Bed

Come, Madam, come, all rest my powers defie,
Until I labour, I in labour lie.
The foe oft-times, having the foe in sight,
Is tired with standing though he never fight.
Off with that girdle, like heavens zone glittering,
But a far fairer world incompassing.
Unpin that spangled breastplate, which you wear
That th'eyes of busie fools may be stopt there:
Unlace your self, for that harmonious chyme
Tells me from you, that now it is bed time.
Off with that happy busk, which I envie,
That still can be, and still can stand so nigh.
Your gown going off, such beauteous state reveals,

As when from flowery meads th'hills shadow steales.
Off with your wyerie Coronet and shew
The haiery Diademe which on you doth grow:
Now off with those shooes, and then safely tread
In this love's hallow'd temple, this soft bed.
In such white robes, heaven's Angels us'd to be
Receavd by men; Thou angel bring'st with thee
A heaven like Mahomets Paradise; and though
Ill spirits walk in white, we easly know
By this these Angels from an evil sprite,
Those set our hairs, but these our flesh upright.

   Licence my roving hands, and let them go
Behind, before, above, between, below.
O my America! my new-found-land,
My kingdome, safeliest when with one man man'd,
My mine of precious stones, My Emperie,
How blest am I in this discovering thee!
To enter in these bonds, is to be free;
Then where my hand is set, my seal shall be.

   Full nakedness! all joyes are due to thee.
As souls unbodied, bodies uncloth'd must be,
To taste whole joyes. Gems which you women use
Are like Atlanta's balls, cast in men's views,
That when a fools eye lighteth on a Gem
His earthly soul may covet theirs, not them.
Like pictures, or like books gay coverings made
For lay-men, are all women thus array'd;
Themselves are mystick books, which only wee
(Whom their imputed grace will dignifie)
Must see reveal'd. Then since that I may know,
As liberally, as to a Midwife, shew
Thy self: cast all, yea, this white lynnen hence,
There is no pennance due to innocence.

   To teach thee, I am naked first; why than
What needst thou have more covering than a man?

Their first child, Constance, was born in early 1603; their second, John, in the spring of 1604. While Donne lived quietly, helping Wolley with estate management and (according to Walton) continuing his studies of civil and canon law, the old Queen died, and with her an old dispensation. James' accession brought with it a rush of benefits and dignities, and many of Donne's acquaintance were promoted or honoured or both. Goodyer was raised to the Privy Chamber; Egerton was made Lord Chancellor and a baron; Donne's father-in-law, Treasurer to the Household of the Prince of Wales; and Sir George's son Robert was knighted, as even was Donne's host, Francis Wolley. Henry Wotton, too, was rewarded. In the manner of a character in a Jacobean play, he had spent the winter of 1601 at the Scottish court disguised as an Italian gentleman with the object of preventing an attempt on James's life. The King, who had been the only one in on the secret of Wotton's identity, showed his gratitude in England by knighting him and sending him to Venice as his ambassador. Donne visited him before he left London, and found him, in relation to the king who had so honoured him:

> *A taper of his torch, a copy writ*
> *From his original, and a fair beam*
> *Of the same warm, and dazzling sun...*

Donne cannot have felt himself warmed by the selfsame sun. Pyrford was the first stop on the royal progress in August 1603; Loseley the second. If Donne was presented to the King on either of these visits (as he almost certainly was), there is no evidence that he sought royal favour. The disgrace of his marriage hung too heavily over him. Two of the most anthologised poems from the *Songs and Sonnets*, 'The Canonization' (see p. 64) and 'The Sun Rising', with their allusions to the King, may belong to Donne's time at Pyrford.

The Sunne Rising

Busie old foole, unruly Sunne,
    Why dost thou thus,
Through windowes, and through curtaines call on us?
Must to thy motions lovers seasons run?
    Sawcy pedantique wretch, goe chide
    Late schoole boyes, and sowre prentices,
  Goe tell Court-huntsmen, that the King will ride,
  Call countrey ants to harvest offices;
Love, all alike, no season knowes, nor clyme,
Nor houres, dayes, moneths, which are the rags of time.

    Thy beames, so reverend, and strong
    Why shouldst thou thinke?
I could eclipse and cloud them with a winke,
But that I would not lose her sight so long:
    f her eyes have not blinded thine,
    Looke, and to morrow late, tell mee,
  Whether both the'India's of spice and Myne
  Be where thou leftst them, or lie here with mee.
Aske for those Kings whom thou saw'st yesterday,
And thou shalt heare, All here in one bed lay.

    She'is all States, and all Princes, I,
    Nothing else is.
Princes doe but play us; compar'd to this,
All honor's mimique; All wealth alchimie.
    Thou sunne art halfe as happy'as wee,
    In that the world's contracted thus;
  Thine age askes ease, and since thy duties bee
  To warme the world, that's done in warming us.
Shine here to us, and thou art every where;
This bed thy center is, these walls, thy spheare.

By 1605, the family's attachment to Wolley may have started to look compromising, Their host was a spendthrift and he had forced his wife to look after the illegitimate child he had had with his mistress. Detaching himself from embarrassing patrons (beginning with Essex) was a pattern Donne followed throughout his life. In February, his name appears with Sir Walter Chute's on a travel permit licensing them to travel for three years with two servant and four 'nagges'. It is not clear what Donne's objectives were. Perhaps he felt a period abroad refreshing his languages and picking up news overseas would improve his secretarial prospects. Almost nothing is known about the journey itself, although allusions in Donne's correspondence in later years imply that he and Chute, a young Kentish gentleman, visited Paris and Venice (where Donne may have met the theologian Paulo Sarpi). The christening of the Donnes' third child, George, in Camberwell would suggest that Ann and the children were left with her sister in Peckham while Donne was away. On his return a rapprochement of some sort was reached with Sir George, who agreed to pay them an income of £80 a year. This allowance probably prompted the family's decision to move into their own house in Mitcham in Surrey, where they were to live from 1606 until 1611.

Blasted with sighs:
Mitcham and London

The cottage Donne lived in at Mitcham was pulled down in the nineteenth century, but a sketch of it survives. A two-storied, gabled house, with an extra wing and a line of yews, it accommodated his growing family for five years. Four children – three girls and one boy – were added to the three they brought with them, and the letters Donne wrote from Mitcham reveal him at his most domesticated:

I write from the fireside in my parlour, and in the noise of three gamesome children; and by the side of her, whom because I have transplanted into a wretched fortune, I must labour to disguise that from her by all such honest devices, as giving her my company, and discourse, therefore I steal from her, all the time which I give to this letter, and it is therefore that I take so short a list, and gallop so fast over it, I have not been out of my house since I received your packet.

Underneath a comforting book-lined study was a damp cellar that perhaps contributed to the series of family sicknesses Donne complains of, and he often described the place in letters as a hospital or dungeon. Donne himself suffered an acute bout of neuritis in 1608, and sought to distract himself by writing his 'Litanie'. His letters in this period are often melancholy, even suicidal. *Biathanatos*, his treatise on suicide (which we will come to later), belongs to this period, and may in part have been written in a spirit of defiance, to face down his demons.

And yet the family was not cut off. Ann Donne had sisters in Peckham and nearby Beddington, and London Bridge was for Donne only a two hours' ride away, and from 1607 to 1611 he kept lodgings on the Strand, somewhere near what is now Bedford Street. He clearly spent a good deal of time in London, keeping in touch with developments at court and seeking some fitting employment for himself, where he was, according to Walton, 'often visited by many of the Nobility and others of this Nation, who used him in their counsels of greatest consideration: and with some rewards for his better subsistence'. Traces of a few of Donne's attempts to gain employment have survived. When a vacancy arose in the Queen's household in June 1607, Sir Henry Goodyer, his chief lifeline to the court, was requested to put in a word for Donne with William Fowler, the Queen's Secretary; in November 1608, he persuaded Lord Hay, one of the royal favourites and a notorious spendthrift, to put him forward for a vacant secretaryship in Ireland; in February 1609 he is reported chasing a secretaryship in the new Virginia Company. Had he succeeded in the last course, he would have joined the ship famously wrecked off Bermuda that supplied Shakespeare with the starting point for *The Tempest*. But his efforts proved un-availing here, as they proved everywhere else. Whenever the subject of Donne's preferment was brought before the King, James recalled the 'worst part of [his] history', the 'disorderly proceedings' of Donne's hasty marriage, and obdurately refused to consider him fit for public office.

More rewarding were the friendships (Donne's 'second reli-gion') he made and developed in these years. Chief of these was with Sir Henry Goodyer, to whom Donne wrote once a week every week whenever they were out of London. Goodyer, who was about Donne's age, had studied in Cambridge and at Gray's Inn. He had been knighted in Ireland by Essex and, under James, was made a Gentleman of the Privy Chamber. Easy-going, cultured, sympathetic and open-handed to a fault, Goodyer was Donne's chief confidant, his disposition to mirth correcting Donne's more saturnine temperament. Both parties were aware of the difference in their fortunes, Goodyer living 'in the Sun' while Donne remained 'but in shadow, which is not no light, but a pallid, waterish and diluted one'. Donne looked to Goodyer for financial and moral support and Goodyer to Donne for his willingness to write brilliantly crafted letters on his behalf. The voice of Donne in his letters to Goodyer is unfailingly thoughtful, considerate, disinterested and candid. Many of Donne's letters are not so much means of conveying news as essays or meditations written for his own and his readers' profit. 'I make account that this writing of letters,' he wrote to Goodyer, 'when it is with any seriousness, is a kind of ecstasy, and a departure and secession and suspension of the soul, which doth then communicate itself to two bodies.' Similar sentiments also characterise the poetry he dedicated to him.

To Sir *Henry Goodyere*

Who makes the Past, a patterne for next yeare,
    Turnes no new leafe, but still the same things reads,
Seene things, he sees againe, heard things doth heare,
    And makes his life, but like a paire of beads.

A Palace, when 'tis that, which it should be,
    Leaves growing, and stands such, or else decayes:
But hee which dwels there, is not so; for hee
    Strives to urge upward, and his fortune raise;

So had your body'her morning, hath her noone,
    And shall not better; her next change is night:
But her faire larger guest, to whom Sun and Moone
    Are sparkes, and short-liv'd, claims another right.

The noble Soule by age grows lustier,
    Her appetite, and her digestion mend,
Wee must not sterve, nor hope to pamper her
    With womens milke, and pappe unto the end.

Provide you manlyer dyet; you have seene
    All libraries, which are Schools, Camps, and Courts;
But aske your Garners if you have not beene
    In harvests, too indulgent to your sports.

Would you redeeme it? then your selfe transplant
    A while from hence. Perchance outlandish ground
Beares no more wit, then ours, but yet more scant
    Are those diversions there, which here abound.

To be a stranger hath that benefit,
    Wee can beginnings, but not habits choke.
Goe; whither? Hence; you get, if you forget;
    New faults, till they prescribe in us, are smoake.

Our soule, whose country'is heaven, and God her father,
    Into this world, corruptions sinke, is sent,
Yet, so much in her travaile she doth gather,
    That she returnes home, wiser than she went;

It payes you well, if it teach you to spare,
    And make you,'asham'd, to make your hawks praise, yours,
Which when herselfe she lessens in the aire,
    You then first say, that high enough she toures.

However, keepe the lively tast you hold
    Of God, love him as now, but fear him more,
And in your afternoones thinke what you told
    And promis'd him, at morning prayer before.

Let falsehood like a discord anger you,
  Else be not froward. But why doe I touch
Things, of which none is in your practise new,
  And Tables, or fruit-trenchers teach as much;

But thus I make you keepe your promise Sir,
  Riding I had you, though you staid still there,
And in these thoughts, although you never stirre,
  You came with mee to Micham, and are here.

This kind of poem, addressed as a gift or tribute to a particular individual, dominated Donne's poetic output for the next ten years or so; gradually, more and more of his poems were written to order. This is never more true than of those he dedicated to Lucy, Countess of Bedford, to whom Donne had been introduced by Goodyer in or around 1607. A Lady of the Queen's Bedchamber, charming, vivacious, a brilliant courtier and performer in the masques of Ben Jonson and Inigo Jones, Lady Bedford possessed rank, youth, wealth, a cultured intelligence and a largely absent husband. For his unwise involvement in the fiasco of the Essex rebellion, the Earl was confined to his estate, leaving his wife an unusual degree of independence. Lady Bedford's natural charm and glamour were unquestionably enhanced by her access to a number of the King's ministers, and in her youth she gathered around herself a literary court, which included Ben Jonson, George Chapman, Samuel Daniel and Michael Drayton as well as Donne. In one of the numerous poems entitled 'To the Countess of Bedford' he described her as 'God's masterpiece' and her friends as 'saints' who had been glorified by her 'election', and many of the poems of his early middle age relate in some (often oblique) way to Lucy. The miraculous 'Air and Angels' has sometimes been associated with Lady Bedford, but in truth without much foundation.

Aire and Angels

Twice or thrice had I loved thee,
Before I knew thy face or name;
So in a voice, so in a shapelesse flame,
Angells affect us oft, and worship'd bee;
  Still when, to where thou wert, I came,
Some lovely glorious nothing I did see.
  But since my soule, whose child love is,
Takes limmes of flesh, and else could nothing doe,
  More subtile then the parent is,
Love must not be, but take a body too,
  And therefore what thou wert, and who
    I bid Love aske, and now
That it assume thy body, I allow,
And fixe it selfe in thy lip, eye, and brow.

Whilst thus to ballast love, I thought,
And so more steddily to have gone,
With wares which would sinke admiration,
I saw, I had loves pinnace overfraught,
  Ev'ry thy haire for love to worke upon
Is much too much, some fitter must be sought;
  For, nor in nothing, nor in things
Extreme, and scatt'ring bright, can love inhere;
  Then as an Angell, face, and wings
Of aire, not pure as it, yet pure doth weare,
  So thy love may be my loves spheare;
    Just such disparitie
As is twixt Aire and Angells puritie,
'Twixt womens love, and mens will ever bee.

Twickenham Park, Lady Bedford's house near Richmond, whose lease had been negotiated by Goodyer in 1607, is the setting for

'Twickenham Garden', one of the most emotionally extreme *Songs and Sonnets*. In one of his letters Donne alludes to some verses Lucy had shown him, and there is the suggestion of secrecy that implies a confidential relationship of some kind – or the hope of one, or the pose of hoping for one – and there is a similar implication in the poem. But whether he ever showed her the poem, or whether the reality or the pose is secret, it is impossible to say. A comparison with a letter to Goodyer written at around the same time yields a revealing insight into the indirect relations between Donne's life and imagination. 'Because I am in a place and season where I see every thing bud forth, I must do too... [yet] the pleasantness of the season displeases me. Everything refreshes, and I wither, and I grow older and not better, my strength diminishes, and my load grows.' In the poem, however, the occasion and cause of this misery has been transferred to disappointed love.

Twicknam Garden

Blasted with sighs, and surrounded with teares,
 Hither I come to seeke the spring,
 And at mine eyes, and at mine eares,
Receive such balmes, as else cure every thing;
  But O, selfe traytor, I do bring
The spider love, which transubstantiates all,
  And can convert Manna to gall,
And that this place may thoroughly be thought
 True Paradise, I have the serpent brought.

'Twere wholsomer for mee, that winter did
 Benight the glory of this place,
 And that a grave frost did forbid
These trees to laugh, and mocke mee to my face;
  But that I may not this disgrace

Indure, nor yet leave loving, Love let mee
  Some senslesse peece of this place bee;
Make me a mandrake, so I may groane here,
  Or a stone fountaine weeping out my yeare.

Hither with christall vyals, lovers come,
  And take my teares, which are loves wine,
  And try your mistresse Teares at home,
For all are false, that tast not just like mine;
  Alas, hearts do not in eyes shine,
Nor can you more judge womans thoughts by teares,
  Then by her shadow, what she weares.
O perverse sexe, where none is true but shee,
  Who's therefore true, because her truth kills mee.

Donne also came into contact with others in the Countess' circle. In May 1609, Lady Bedford's cousin, Lady Markham, died at Twickenham at the age of thirty, and drew from Donne a rather frigid elegy; three months later, he wrote another in memory of her friend Cecelia Bulstrode. But Lady Bedford's patronage was not exclusive and occasionally got him into difficulties. Goodyer urged him to write some dedicatory verses to Lady Huntingdon, which he did in the awkward consciousness of the 'integrity' he owed 'the other Countess'. He feared that if the verses he wrote to Lady Huntingdon were as fervent as those he wrote to Lady Bedford he would lose her friendship and the prospect of her patronage.

The potential embarrassment was probably greater with regard to another of Donne's major patrons, Mrs Magdalen Herbert, whose acquaintance the poet renewed in 1607 – some eight years after their first meeting in Oxford. Five years older than Donne and a widow, she was certainly the recipient of the sonnet 'Of Mary Magdalene' and might or might not have been the object of a number of the *Songs and Sonnets*. Both 'The

Relique' (see p. 9) and 'The Funeral' have been associated with her, neither for any very good reason, except for the reference to the Magdalen and the suggestion of her reputation for golden hair in the line 'a bracelet of bright hair about the bone'.

The Funerall

Who ever comes to shroud me, do not harme
    Nor question much
That subtile wreath of haire, which crowns my arme;
The mystery, the signe you must not touch,
    For 'tis my outward Soule,
Viceroy to that, which then to heaven being gone,
    Will leave this to controule,
And keepe these limbes, her Provinces, from dissolution.

For if the sinewie thread my braine lets fall
    Through every part,
Can tye those parts, and make mee one of all;
These haires which upward grew, and strength and art
    Have from a better braine,
Can better do'it; Except she meant that I
    By this should know my pain,
As prisoners then are manacled, when they'are condemn'd to die.

What ere shee meant by'it, bury it with me,
    For since I am
Loves martyr, it might breed idolatrie,
If into others hands these Reliques came;
    As'twas humility
To afford to it all that a Soule can doe,
    So, 'tis some bravery,
That since you would save none of mee, I bury some of you.

There is more reason to identify (as Walton does) Magdalen Herbert as the subject of his elegy 'The Autumnall' (see p. 56), although it seems unlikely that she would have been pleased with being referred to as fifty rather than forty – or even thirty-two, if the poem did arise from a first meeting in Oxford in 1599. Walton insisted that theirs 'was not an amity that polluted their souls'. In the end, any real or pretended subject seems unimportant, because, as with 'Twickenham Garden', it is Donne himself who occupies the centre of the poem. Mrs Herbert was also the recipient of 'La Corona', the series of devotional sonnets and Donne's first experiment in explicitly religious poetry.

I

Deigne at my hands this crown of prayer and praise,
Weav'd in my low devout melancholie,
Thou which of good, hast, yea art treasury,
All changing unchang'd Antient of dayes,
But doe not, with a vile crowne of fraile bayes,
Reward my muses white sincerity,
But what thy thorny crowne gain'd, that give mee,
A crowne of glory. which doth flower alwayes;
The ends crowne our workes, but thou crown'st our ends,
For, at our end begins our endless rest,
This first last end, now zealously possessed
ith a strong sober thirst, my soul attends.
'Tis time that heart and voice be lifted high,
Salvation to all that will is nigh.

Salvation to all that will is nigh.

Donne also came across her son, Sir Edward Herbert, later Lord Herbert of Cherbury, almost certainly at the Herbert family's house near Charing Cross. This Herbert was the first of Donne's literary followers, and almost certainly the recipient of 'The Primrose' and perhaps 'The Ecstasy'.

The Extasie

Where, like a pillow on a bed,
  A Pregnant banke swelled up, to rest
The violets reclining head,
  Sat we two, one another's best;
Our hands were firmly cimented
  With a fast balme, which thence did spring,
Our eye-beames twisted, and did thred
  Our eyes, upon one double string;
So to'entergraft our hands, as yet
  Was all the meanes to make us one,
And pictures in our eyes to get
  Was all our propagation.
As 'twixt two equal Armies, Fate
Suspends uncertaine victorie,
Our soules, (which to advance their state,
Were gone out), hung 'twixt her, and mee.
And whil'st our souls negotiate there,
Wee like sepulchrall statues lay;
All day, the same our postures were,
  And wee said nothing, all the day.
If any, so by love refin'd,
  That he soules language understood,
And by good love were growen all minde,
  Within convenient distance stood,
He (though he knew not which soule spake
  Because both meant, both spake the same)

Might thence a new concoction take,
    And part farre purer than he came.
This Extasie doth unperplex
    (We said) and tell us what we love,
Wee see by this, it was not sexe,
    We see, we saw not what did move.
But as all several soules containe
    Mixture of things, they not what,
Love, these mixt soules doth mixe againe,
    And makes both one, each this and that.
A single violet transplant,
    The strength, the colour, and the size,
(All which before was poore, and scant,)
    Redoubles still, and multiplies.
When love, with one another so
    Interinanimates two soules,
That abler soule, which thence doth flow,
    Defects of lonelinesse controules.
Wee then, who are this new soule, know,
    Of what we are compos'd, and made,
For, th'Atomies of which we grow,
    Are soules, whom no change can invade.
But O alas, so long, so farre
    Our bodies why doe wee forbeare?
They'are ours, though they'are not wee, Wee are
    The intelligences, they the spheare.
We owe them thankes, because they thus,
    Did us, to us, at first convay,
Yeelded their forces, sense, to us,
    Nor are drosse to us, but allay.
On man heavens influence workes not so,
    But that it first imprints the ayre,
Soe soule into the soule may flow,
    Though it to body first repaire.
As our blood labours to beget

Spirits, as like soules as it can,
Because such fingers need to knit
That subtile knot, which makes us man:
So must pure lovers soules descend
T' affections, and to faculties,
Which sense may reach and apprehend,
Else a great Prince in prison lies.
To'our bodies turn wee then, that so
Weake men on love reveal'd may looke;
Loves mysteries in soules do grow,
But yet the body is his booke.
And if some lover, such as wee,
Have heard this dialogue of one,
Let him still marke us, he shall see
Small change, when we'are to bodies gone.

Donne's visits to London also took him to convivial literary gatherings. A dog-Latin poem of 1611 celebrating a meeting at the Mitre tavern in Fleet Street and including a mock eulogy to the travel writer Thomas Coryate, bears Donne's name, beside those of (among others) Sir Henry Goodyer, Christopher Brooke and Inigo Jones. A fine was levied against absent friends, and the group constituted a dining club of sorts. In 1612, Coryate, travelling in India, wrote to an acquaintance in London and begged to be remembered to 'the High Seneschall of the right Worshipful Fraternity of Sireniacal Gentlemen, that meet the first Friday of every month, at the sign of the Mermaid in Bread Street in London'. There follows in the postscript a long list of friends to whom Coryate sent his greetings, including Donne and Ben Jonson. Many dining clubs probably met at the Mermaid, so it doesn't follow that Donne attended the battles of wits and heard or spoke the words eulogised by Francis Beaumont in his verse letter to Jonson – words...

So nimble, and so full of subtle flame,
As if that every one (from whence they came)
Had meant to put his whole wit in a jest,
And had resolved to live a fool the rest
Of his dull life…

… but he seems to have belonged to something quite similar.

These friendly gatherings should be remembered when considering the less convivial work with which Donne was also occupied for much of the time while living at Mitcham. This was the composition of his three controversial prose works, *Pseudo-Martyr*, *Ignatius his Conclave* and *Biathanatos*.

Donne's involvement in the controversies of canon law was encouraged by his association with Thomas Morton, Dean of Gloucester, one of James' most effective hammers against Jesuitism. Soon after his appointment to the Deanery in June 1607, Morton summoned Donne and tried to persuade him to join the Church by offering him a benefice that had come with his job. 'At the hearing of this,' in Walton's quite dramatic report of the interview, 'Mr Donne's faint breath and perplexed countenance gave a visible testimony of an inward conflict.' After three days' thought, Donne returned to Morton to decline the offer. In his words, as Walton reports them, 'Some irregularities of my life have been so visible to some men, that though I have, I thank God, made my peace with him by penitential resolutions against them… yet this… is not so visible to man, as to free me from their censures, and it may be that sacred calling from a dishonour.' In other words, the blot of his marriage and perhaps the rumours of a racy youth, were held up as reasons not to enter the Church. But if Donne did not take up Morton's offer, he kept in regular contact with him. He seems to have read and commented on the Dean's work before publication, and probably recognised the potential advantages to himself of taking the royal side in the pamphlet wars that raged over the disagreements between the churches of England and Rome.

The first two of Donne's controversial works grew, as Walton writes, out of his 'constant study of some points of controversy betwixt the English and Roman Church; and especially those of supremacy and allegiance'. After the failure of the gunpowder plot in 1605, one of Parliament's immediate actions was to impose a new Oath of Allegiance, whereby all Roman Catholics were required to acknowledge James as their lawful sovereign, to deny the power of the Pope to depose him or authorise any other sovereign to invade his kingdom or to release his subjects from this allegiance. In intemperate language it also required every king's subject to swear that he did 'from his heart abhor, detest, and abjure, as impious and heretical, this damnable doctrine and position, that princes which be excommunicated or deprived by the Pope may be deposed or murdered by their subjects'. Notwithstanding this rather inflammatorily tone, its aim, James maintained, was to establish a 'true distinction between papists of quiet disposition, and in all other things good subjects, and such other papists as in their hearts maintained the like violent bloody maxims, that the powder-traitors did'.

Chief among those who opposed the Oath was the Jesuit, Robert Persons, a formidably skilful and ironic stylist (later much admired by Swift). When Persons' pamphlet *Judgement of a Catholic Englishman living in banishment for his religion… concerning a late book set forth, and entitled, Triplici nodo, triplex cuneus* appeared in 1608, condemning the Oath and ridiculing James' denial that he was a heretic, the King engaged William Barlow, the Bishop of Lincoln and Jacobean England's answer to the insinuatingly ambitious Obadiah Slope of Trollope's *Barchester Towers*, to defend him. Barlow's unctuousness didn't qualify him as an effective controversialist and his reply, *Answer to a Catholic Englishman*, published in April 1609, fell very flat – and the Jesuits fell upon it. A letter from Donne to Goodyer gives us his own opinion of Barlow's feeble effort. It was a book, he wrote:

... full of falsifications in words, and in sense, and of falsehoods in matter of fact, and of inconsequent and unscholarlike arguings, and of relinquishing the King, in many points of defence, and of contradiction of himself, and of dangerous and suspected Doctrine in Divinity, and of silly ridiculous triflings, and of extreme flatteries, and of neglecting better and more obvious answers, and of letting slip some enormous advantages which the other gave, and he spies not.

Such was the background against which Donne wrote his *Pseudo-Martyr*, published in January 1610, and written, according to Walton, in a mere six weeks. (He also states that the book was written at the King's command, but this is probably an exaggeration, and the title page makes no such claim.) The basis of Donne's argument was twofold: first, that Catholics in England should take the Oath of Allegiance, and second that anyone who refused to do so had no right to proclaim him or herself a marytr, or to be proclaimed one. The weight he places on the second half of his case reflects eloquently Donne's Catholic upbringing – one, as he writes in *Pseudo-Martyr*, that had 'been ever kept awake in a meditation of Martyrdom'. His own experience therefore led him to soften (and harden) the tone of the book where required. To the wavering and nervous Roman Catholic, he was sympathetic; towards the hard-line Jesuit, vitriolic, referring to the Society of Jesus as 'an ordinary instrument of [the devil], (whose continual libels and incitatory books, have occasioned more afflictions and drawn more of that blood, which they call Catholic, in this Kingdom, than all our Acts of Parliament have done)'.

The prodigious display of learning with which Donne marshalled his arguments and the attitude he adopted, by turns combative and conciliatory, greatly raised his stock in some circles, and there is no doubt that this intervention in the theological fray was in some measure calculated and opportunistic.

While the book was still warm from the press, Donne travelled to Royston in Hertfordshire, where the King was hunting, and presented him with a copy. James was impressed, in fact too impressed, because if Donne was hoping (as he certainly was) to be rewarded with a senior secular position of some kind, he was to be, once again, disappointed. As Walton wrote, 'When the King had read and considered that Book, he persuaded Mr Donne to enter into the ministry.' Its author may have been mollified by the honorary MA it earned him from Oxford (he had never received a degree from either university) but in terms of his career, *Pseudo-Martyr* was a spectacular backfire.

The pamphlet *Ignatius his Conclave*, which followed *Pseudo-Martyr* at the end of the same year, is written in a less temperate, more satirical vein, and may include some of the less scholarly material Donne felt he couldn't include in *Pseudo-Martyr*. Its object is to lampoon and satirise the Jesuits, whose spokesman, St Ignatius, is so quarrelsome in Hell that Lucifer creates a special home for him and his fellow Jesuits on the moon. It also reveals Donne's impatience with the religious disputes of his times and ridicules Christian controversy itself.

Ignatius was a success, being rapidly reprinted in the year following its publication, and going through several later editions in both English and Latin. Nevertheless, in spite of entering the lists of controversy, and still moving within quite elevated social and intellectual circles, Donne was often depressed at the directionless quality of his life. In his letters a Hamlet-like melancholy and self-disgust, and a sense of detachedness (reminiscent here of the words of his most famous meditation), afflicted him: 'I would fain do something; but that I cannot tell what, is no wonder. For to choose, is to do: but to be no part of any body, is to be nothing. At most, the greatest persons, are but great wens, and excrescences; men of wit and delightful conversation, but as moles for ornament, except they be so incorporated into the body of the world, that they contribute something to the sustentation of the whole.'

His greatest poetic expression of this mood of 'nothingness' is found in another poem, 'A Nocturnal upon S. *Lucies* Day' (see p. 120), which may superficially be connected with another Lucy, the Countess of Bedford. But since its date is unknown, in what way it may relate to her, or his wife, or another, or a fictional 'she' is indecipherable. Wherever the poem belongs in Donne's career, it suggests the mood in which he had approached another of the controversial works of his Mitcham years. *Biathanatos* ('violent death' in Greek), which was probably written in 1608, is Donne's defence of suicide. And while the tone of the argument may be intellectually earnest, abstruse and legalistic, its origins were personal, as the preface makes clear:

> I have often such a sickly inclination. And, whether it be because I had my first breeding and conversation with men of a suppressed and afflicted Religion, accustomed to the despite of death, and hungry of an imagin'd Martyrdom; or that the common Enemy find that door worst locked against him in me; or that there be a perplexity and flexibility in the doctrine itself; or because my conscience ever assures me, that no rebellious grudging at God's gifts, nor other sinful concurrence accompanies these thoughts in me, or that a brave scorn, or that faint cowardliness beget it, whensoever any affliction assails me, me thinks I have the keys of my prison in mine own hand, and no remedy presents itself so soon to my heart, as mine own sword.

Writing it was in some measure a therapeutic exercise.

It may have been a response to a question that was in the air – Hamlet's question – but *Biathanatos* was nevertheless the first book about suicide to be written in English. The context of Donne's inquiry, unlike the largely Stoic context of Montaigne's discussion of suicide in his essay 'A custom of the Isle of Cea', is entirely Christian. By dividing the book into three parts, which consider in turn the objections of nature, reason and the law of

God, Donne was tackling arguments put forward by St Augustine in the *City of God*. He attacks the entrenched, pitiless position of the church, which endorsed the standard treatment of the self-murderer – which was to be dragged through towns with a stake through the body and buried at a crossroads. At its heart is the controversial suggestion, obliquely made, that Christ himself, who elected to die a voluntary death 'which was his own act, and before his natural time', committed suicide.

Biathanatos is unequivocal in defending the individual conscience against the prescriptions of the Church – a position somewhat at variance to that adopted by Donne after he was ordained (although not when it came to suicide), but it is not always easy to discern his purposes. It contains a streak of moral relativism that rendered it too heterodox for publication. It was written for circulation among friends, and the university men to whom Donne showed it pronounced that 'certainly there was a false thread in it, but not easily found'. Donne clearly felt that, like his poetry, it would be best not to broadcast it too widely – a conviction he still held some ten or eleven years later, when he handed it over to his friend Sir Robert Ker for safekeeping, and asked him to 'Reserve it for me, if I live, and if I die, I only forbid it the press, and the fire: publish it not, but yet burn it not; and between these, do what you will with it.'

The deepening religious seriousness of Donne's thought, and the feelings of despair that accompanied it, found their most famous and urgent expression in the *Holy Sonnets*, which almost certainly do not belong to Donne's later years as a divine (as was once thought) but to the rootless, anxious years he divided between London and Mitcham. His conviction of personal failure and a sense of being out of things may have provided the immediate background, but they articulate more universal fears. They are like entries in the journal of a solitary soul, divorced from a spiritual community once provided by the old faith, when all that was required of the believer was that he or she follow the sacraments and services of the Roman Catholic Church. The poems confront the new spiritual responsibilities demanded by Protestantism and come face to face with the excruciating possibility that Calvinism – the doctrine that salvation was predestined for a spiritual elect – might be true. The order and numbering (in brackets) given to the sonnets here follow modern thinking about their order of composition. The numbering in Grierson's edition is given in Roman numerals. The first six may have been written for the Earl of Dorset, an admirer of Donne's poetry and a patron recently introduced to Donne through Goodyer, but their Calvinism also suggests they may have been written for Lady Bedford, whose religious persuasion increasingly lay that way.

VI [3]

This is my playes last scene, here heavens appoint
My pilgrimages last mile; and my race
Idly, yet quickly runne, hath this last pace,
My spans last inch, my minutes latest point,
And gluttonous death, will instantly unjoynt
My body, and soule, and I shall sleepe a space,
But my'ever-waking part shall see that face,
Whose feare already shakes my every joynt:
Then, as my soule, to'heaven her first seate, takes flight,
And earth-borne body, in the earth shall dwell,
So, fall my sinnes, that all may have their right,
To where they'are bred, and would presse me, to hell.
Impute me righteous, thus purg'd of evill,
For thus I leave the world, the flesh, and devill.

VII [4]

At the round earths imagin'd corners, blow
Your trumpets, Angells, and arise, arise
From death, you numberlesse infinities

Of soules, and to your scattred bodies goe,
All whom the flood did, and fire shall o'erthrow,
All whom warre, dearth, age, agues, tyrannies,
Despaire, law, chance, hath slaine, and you whose eyes,
Shall behold God, and never tast deaths woe.
But let them sleepe, Lord, and mee mourne a space,
For, if above all these, my sinnes abound,
'Tis late to ask abundance of thy grace,
When wee are there; here on this lowly ground,
Teach mee how to repent; for that's as good
As if thou'hadst seal'd my pardon, with thy blood.

X [6]

Death be not proud, though some have called thee
Mighty and dreadfull, for, thou art not soe,
For, those, whom thou think'st, thou dost overthrow,
Die not, poore death, nor yet canst thou kill mee.
From rest and sleepe, which but thy pictures bee,
Much pleasure, then from thee, much more must flow,
And soonest our best men with thee doe goe,
Rest of our bones, and soules deliverie.
Thou art slave to Fate, Chance, kings, and desperate men,
And dost with poyson, warre, and sicknesse dwell,
And poppie, or charmes can make us sleepe as well,
And better than thy stroake; why swell'st thou then?
One short sleepe past, wee wake eternally,
And death shall be no more, death thou shalt die.

XI [7]

Spit in my face you Jewes, and pierce my side,
Buffet, and scoffe, scourge, and crucifie mee,
For I have sinn'd, and sinn'd, and onely hee,
Who could do no iniquitie, hath died:
But by my death cannot be satisfied

My sinnes, which passe the Jewes impiety:
They kill'd once an inglorious man, but I
Crucifie him daily, being now glorified.
Oh let mee then, his strange love still admire:
Kings pardon, but he bore our punishment.
And Jacob came cloth'd in vile harsh attire
But to supplant, and with gainfull intent:
God cloth'd himselfe in vile mans flesh, that so
Hee might be weake enough to suffer woe.

XIII [9]

What if this present were the worlds last night?
Marke in my heart, O soul, where thou dost dwell,
The picture of Christ crucified, and tell
Whether that countenance can thee affright,
Teares in his eyes quench the amazing light,
Blood fills his frownes, which from his pierc'd head fell,
And can that tongue adjuge thee unto hell,
Which pray'd forgivenesse for his foes fierce spight?
No, no; but as in my idolatrie
I said to all my profane mistresses,
Beauty, of pity, foulnesse onely is
A signe of rigour: so say I to thee,
To wicked spirits are horrid shapes assign'd,
This beauteous forme assures a pitious minde.

XIV [10]

Batter my heart, three-person'd God; for, you
As yet but knocke, breathe, shine, and seeke to mend;
That I may rise, and stand, o'erthrow me, and bend
Your force, to breake, blowe, burn, and make me new.
I, like an usurpt town, to'another due,
Labour to'admit you, but Oh, to no end,
Reason your viceroy in mee, mee should defend,

But is captiv'd, and proves weake or untrue,
Yet dearly'I love you,'and would be loved faine,
But am betroth'd unto your enemie:
Divorce mee,'untie, or breake that knot againe,
Take mee to you, imprison mee, for I
Except you'enthrall me, never shall be free,
Nor ever chast, except you ravish mee.

I [13]

Thou hast made me, and shall thy worke decay?
Repair me now, for mine end doth haste,
I runne to death, and death meets me as fast,
And all my pleasures are like yesterday;
I dare not move my dimme eyes any way,
Despaire behind, and death before doth cast
Such terrour, and my feeble flesh doth waste
By sinne in it, which it t'wards hell doth weigh;
Onely thou art above, and when towards thee
By thy leave I can looke, I rise againe;
But our old subtle foe so tempteth me,
That not one houre I can my selfe sustaine;
Thy Grace may wing me to prevent his art,
And thou like Adamant draw mine iron heart.

V [15]

I am a little world made cunningly
Of elements, and an Angelike spright,
But black sinne hath betrayed to endless night
My worlds both parts, and (oh) both parts must die.
You which beyond that heaven which was most high
Have found new sphears, and of new lands can write,
Powre new seas in mine eyes, that so I might
Drowne my world with my weeping earnestly,
Or wash it, if it must be drown'd no more:

But oh it must be burnt! alas the fire
Of lust and envie have burnt it heretofore,
And made it fouler; Let their flames retire,
And burne me o Lord, with a fiery zeale
Of thee and thy house, which doth in eating heale.

VIII [16]

If faithful soules be alike glorifi'd
As Angels, then my father's soule doth see,
And adds this even to full felicity,
That valiantly I hell's wide mouth o'erstride:
But if our mindes to these soules be descry'd
By circumstances, and by signes that be
Apparent in us, not immediately,
How shall my mindes white truth by them be try'd?
They see idolatrous lovers weepe and mourne,
And vile blasphemous Conjurers to call
On Jesus name, and Pharisaicall
Dissemblers feigne devotion. Then turne
O pensive soule, to God, for he knowes best
Thy true griefe, for he put it in my breast.

My soul's form bends toward the east:
The Drurys and Drury Lane

In early 1611, Donne found himself a new patron in the figure of Sir Robert Drury, a Gentleman of the King's Chamber, who had turned from soldiering to diplomacy – or at least, diplomacy was what he aspired to. Donne's acquaintance with Drury may have begun during their years together at Cambridge in the late 1580s, or perhaps during the expedition against Cadiz. He may also have known or come to know him better through his sister, whose husband William Lyly had served under Drury's uncle and later settled in Hawstead in Suffolk, where he received the patronage of the family.

In December 1610, tragedy had struck the Drurys with the death of their fourteen-year-old daughter, Elizabeth. It may well have been Anne Donne who, with a view to getting her brother a new patron, suggested that he present the grief-stricken parents with an elegy on her death. The fact that Donne had never met Elizabeth Drury proved no impediment to his imagination.

A Funerall Elegie

'Tis lost, to trust a Tombe with such a guest,
Or to confine her in a marble chest.
Alas, what's Marble, Jeat, or Porphyrie,

Priz'd with the Chrysolite of either eye,
Or with those Pearles, and Rubies, which she was?
Joyne the two Indies in one Tombe, 'tis glass;
And so is all to her materials,
Though every inch were ten Escurials,
Yet she's demolish'd: can wee keepe her then
In works of hands, or of the wits of men?
Can these memorials, ragges of paper, give
Life to that name, by which name they must live?
Sickly, alas, short-liv'd, aborted bee
Those carcasse verses, whose soule is not shee.
And can shee, who no longer would be shee,
Being such a Tabernacle, stoop to be
In paper wrapt; or, when shee would not lie
In such a house, dwell in an Elegie?
But 'tis no matter; wee may well allow
Verse to live so long as the world will now.
For her death wounded it. The world containes
Princes for armes, and Counsellors for braines,
Lawyers for tongues, Divines for hearts, and more,
The Rich for stomackes, and for backes, the Poore;
The Officers for hands, Merchants for feet
By which remote and distant Countries meet.
But those fine spirits which do tune, and set
This Organ, are those pieces which beget
Wonder and love; and these were shee; and shee
Being spent, the world must needs decrepit be.
For since death will proceed to triumph still,
He can finde nothing, after her, to kill,
Except the world it selfe, so great as shee.
Thus brave and confident may Nature bee,
Death cannot give her such another blow,
Because shee cannot such another show.
But must wee say she's dead? may't not be said
That as a sundred clock is peecemeale laid,

Not to be lost, but by the makers hand
Repollish'd, without errour then to stand,
Or as the Affrique Niger streame enwombs
It selfe into the earth, and after comes
(Having first made a naturall bridge, to passe
For many leagues) farre greater than it was,
May't not be said, that her grave shall restore
Her, greater, purer, firmer, then before?...

The gesture paid off. Sir Robert and Lady Drury were greatly moved, and on coming to know each other better Donne and Drury discovered that they had more than a university education and a military career in common: both were, by the standards of the day, widely travelled, and both had pursued diplomatic appointments overseas without success. In addition to his many other abilities, it may well have been Donne's facility in foreign languages that prompted Drury to invite him to join his family on a prolonged continental journey. His job would be to assist Drury in drafting informal reports on developments overseas. The trip would give Donne the opportunity to keep abreast of developments on the Continent and fix his attention on the conditions of Protestants abroad. He accepted, and on 2nd July 1611 a permit was granted to Sir Robert to travel 'with his wife and family, for three years, with twelve horses, coach and fifty pounds in money'.

Drury's invitation did not go down well at Mitcham. Ann was (as often) pregnant, unwell and, according to Walton:

... professed an unwillingness to allow [Donne] any absence from her; saying, her divining soul boded her some ill in his absence; and therefore, desired him not to leave her. This made Mr Donne lay aside all thoughts of the journey, and really to resolve against it. But Sir Robert became restless in his persuasions for it; and Mr Donne was so generous, as to think he had sold his liberty when he received so many charitable kindnesses from him: and told his wife so; who did therefore with an unwilling-willingness give a faint consent to the journey.

He might go for two months, but be back for the birth. If Walton is to be believed, their parting inspired two of the most famous *Songs and Sonnets*. The suggestion is appealing, but as so often there is little evidence (internal or external) to corroborate it.

Song

Sweetest love, I do not goe,
For wearinesse of thee,
Nor in hope the world can show
A fitter Love for mee;
But since that I
Must dye at last, 'tis best,
To use my selfe in jest
Thus by fain'd deaths to dye.

Yesternight the Sunne went hence,
And yet is here to day,
He hath no desire nor sense,
Nor halfe so short a way:
Then feare not mee,
But beleeve that I shall make
Speedier journeyes, since I take
More wings and spurres than hee.

O how feeble is mans power,
That if good fortune fall,
Cannot add another houre,
Nor a lost houre recall!

But come bad chance,
  And wee joyne to'it our strength,
  And wee teach it art and length,
    It selfe o'r us to'advance.

When thou sigh'st, thou sigh'st not winde,
  But sigh'st my soule away,
When thou weep'st, unkindly kinde,
  My lifes blood doth decay.
    It cannot bee
That thou lov'st me, as thou say'st,
If in thine my life thou waste,
  Thou art the best of mee.

Let not thy divining heart
  Forethinke me any ill,
Destiny may take thy part,
  And may thy feares fulfill;
    But thinke that wee
Are but turn'd aside to sleepe;
They who one another keepe
  Alive, ne'er parted bee.

A Valediction: forbidding mourning

As virtuous men passe mildly away,
  And whisper to their soules, to goe,
Whilst some of their sad friends doe say,
  The breath goes now, and some say, no:

So let us melt, and make no noise,
  No teare-floods, nor sigh-tempests move,
T'were prophanation of our joyes
  To tell the layetie our love.

Moving of th'earth brings harmes and feares,
    Men reckon what it did and meant,
Bur trepidation of the spheares,
    Though greater farre, is innocent.

Dull sublunary lovers' love
    (Whose soule is sense) cannot admit
Absence, because it doth remove
    Those things which elemented it.

But we by a love, so much refin'd,
    That our selves know not what it is,
Inter-assured of the mind,
    Care lesse, eyes, lips, and hands to misse.

Our two soules therefore, which are one,
    Though I must goe, endure not yet
A breach, but an expansion,
    Like gold to ayery thinnesse beate.

If they be two, they are two so
    As stiffe twin compasses are two,
Thy soule the fixt foot, makes no show
    To move, but doth, if the'other doe.

And though it in the center sit,
    Yet when the other far doth roam,
It leanes, and hearkens after it,
    And growes erect, as that comes home.

Such wilt thou be to mee, who must
    Like th'other foot, obliquely runne;
Thy firmnes makes my circle just,
    And makes me end, where I begunne.

Donne's journey with Drury marks the end of the family's association with Mitcham. Before he left, he sent Ann and the children to live with Frances, her younger sister, now living at Nunwell on the Isle of Wight. Donne seems not to have spent time there while waiting for Drury to finish his business in England, but to have remained in London before embarking, which is where he probably wrote 'An Anatomy of the World', a further poem occasioned by the death of Elizabeth Drury (by now dead 'some months'), 'wherein... the frailty and decay of this whole world is represented.' By the time Donne was persuaded to publish the poem in late 1611, which he did with reluctance and later regret, nearly a year had elapsed since the family had lost their daughter, which explains its second, better-known, title 'The First Anniversary'. It is an autopsy of a dead world; an exorbitant, baroque performance. This passage begins at line 201.

An Anatomy of the World
The first Anniversary

So did the world from the first houer decay,
That evening was beginning of the day,
And now the Springs and Sommers which we see,
Like sonnes of women after fiftie bee.
And new Philosophy calls all in doubt,
The Element of fire is quite put out;
The Sun is lost, and th'earth, and no mans wit
Can well direct him where to looke for it.
And freely men confesse, that this world's spent,
When in the Planets, and the Firmament
They seeke so many new; they see that this
Is crumbled out again to his Atomies.
'Tis all in peeces, all cohaerence gone;
All just supply, and all Relation:
Prince, Subject, Father, Son, are things forgot,

For every man alone thinkes he hath got
To be a Phoenix, and that then can bee
None of that kinde, of which he is, but hee.
This is the worlds condition now, and now
She that should all parts to reunion bow,
She that had all Magnetique force alone,
To draw, and fasten sundred parts in one;
She whom wise nature had invented then
When she observ'd that every sort of men
Did in their voyage in this worlds Sea stray,
And needed a new compasse for their way;
She that was best, and first originall
Of all faire copies; and the generall
Steward to Fate; she whose rich eyes, and brest,
Guilt the West Indies, and perfum'd the East;
Whose having breath'd in this world, did bestow
Spice on those Isles, and bad them still smell so,
And that rich Indie which doth gold interre,
Is but as single money, coyn'd from her:
She to whom this world must it selfe refer,
As Suburbs, or the Microcosme of her,
Shee, shee is dead; shee's dead: when thou knowst this,
Thou knowst how lame a cripple this world is.
And learn'st thus much by our Anatomy,
That this worlds generall sicknesse doth not lie
In any humour, or one certaine part;
But, as thou sawest it rotten at the heart,
Thou seest a Hectique feaver hath got hold
Of the whole substance, not to be contrould,
And that thou hast but one way, not t'admit
The worlds infection, to be none of it.
For the worlds subtilst immateriall parts
Feele this consuming wound, and ages darts.
For the worlds beauty is decai'd, or gone,
Beauty, that's colour, and proportion…

By November, the Drurys were at last ready to set out, and Donne wrote in sombre mood to Sir Henry Goodyer that, 'I am now in the afternoon of my life, and then it is unwholesome to sleep. It is ill to look back, or give over in a course; but worse never to set out. I speak to you at this time of departing, as I should do at my last upon my death-bed.' By 4th December the party – which included coach and horses, riders, servants, hounds and hawks – had reached Amiens. He was not pleased by the town, soon complaining of it in letters as barren and dull, although, by writing the second of the *Anniversaries* there, he created some diversion for himself. This companion piece, even longer than the first and as extravagantly pessimistic, he entitled 'Of the Progress of the Soul' (not to be confused with the unfinished epic of ten years earlier). He may have begun the poem on the exact anniversary of Elizabeth Drury's death. Like the First Anniversary, it is a deliberate exercise in overdriven hyperbole. As elegies to a dead child, both poems are, in John Carey's words, 'about as touching as a brass band'. These are the opening lines:

OF THE PROGRESSE OF THE SOULE
The second Anniversarie

Nothing could make me sooner to confesse
That his world had an everlastingnesse,
Than to consider, that a yeare is runne,
Since both this lower world's, and the Sunnes Sunne,
The Lustre, and the vigor of this All,
Did set; 'twere blasphemie, to say, did fall.
But as a ship which hath strooke saile, doth runne,
By force of that force which before, it wonne:
Or as sometimes in a beheaded man,
Though at those two Red seas, which freely ranne,
One from the Trunke, another from the Head,
His soule be sail'd, to her eternall bed,

His eyes will twinckle, and his tongue will roll,
As though he beckned, and cal'd backe his soule,
He graspes his hands, and he pulls up his feet,
And seemes to reach, and to step forth to meete
His soul; when all these motions which we saw,
Are but as Ice, which crackles at a thaw:
Or as a Lute, which in moist weather, rings
Her knell alone, by cracking of her strings:
So struggles this dead world, now she is gone;
For there is motion in corruption…

On its completion, Donne sent the poem to England, where it was published with a second edition of 'An Anatomy of the World' as the *First and Second Anniversaries*. In March 1612, the party moved to Paris, where Donne took to his sick bed, suffering from 'such storms of a stomach colic as kept me in a continual vomiting'. It was in Paris that he learned of the reception among his English friends and patrons to the publication of his *Anniversaries*. Ben Jonson was not alone in thinking their adulation of a dead girl 'profane and full of blasphemies'. An unfinished verse epistle, written by Donne in Paris and addressed to Lady Bedford, reveals his anxiety that the extravagant praise he had heaped upon Elizabeth Drury in print would mar his relations with the Lady.

This embarrassment was soon put out of Donne's mind by his far greater anxiety for the safety of his wife, of whom he had received no news for some weeks. He was, as he put it in a letter to Goodyer, ignorant as to whether he had been 'increased by a child, or diminished by the loss of a wife'. According to Walton it was at this time that Donne witnessed the apparition of his wife, and reports him as saying to Drury,

I have seen my dear wife pass twice by me through this room, with her hair hanging about her shoulders, and a dead child in her arms: this, I have seen since I saw you. To which Sir Robert replied; Sure Sir, you have slept since I saw you; and, this is the result of some melancholy dream, which I desire you to forget, for you are now awake. To which Mr Donne's reply was: I cannot be surer that I now live, then [sic.] that I have not slept since I saw you: and am, as sure, that at her second appearing, she stopt, and look't me in the face, and vanisht.

A messenger was sent to London and returned after twelve days to report that Ann Donne had given birth to a still-born child at just the time the apparition appeared to her husband. Modern biographers dispute the dramatic neatness of Walton's timing.

The Apparition

When by thy scorne, O murderesse, I am dead,
And that thou thinkst thee free
From all solicitation from mee,
Then shall my ghost come to thy bed,
And thee, feign'd vestal, in worse armes shall see;
Then thy sicke taper will begin to winke,
And he, whose thou art then, being tyr'd before,
Will, if thou stirre, or pinch to wake him, thinke
    Thou call'st for more,
And in false sleepe will from thee shrinke,
And then poore Aspen wretch, neglected thou
Bath'd in a cold quicksilver sweat wilt lye
    A veryer ghost than I:
What I will say, I will not tell thee now,
Lest that preserve thee'; and since my love is spent,
I'had rather thou shouldst painfully repent,
Then by my threatenings rest still innocent.

Later in the same month, public announcement was made of the double betrothal made between Louis XIII with a Spanish Infanta and of Louis' sister with the heir to the throne of Spain. This was accompanied by sumptuous parades and pageants in Paris, all of which Donne received with cool indifference.

In April, the party moved on to Frankfurt and Heidelberg, where Sir Robert took umbrage at the reception he received from the Dowager Electress, which he did not find 'as in his vanity he expected'. Part of Donne's commission was to write thank-you letters on the Drurys' behalf and one relating to their visit, to the Duchesse de Bouillon, survives in his handwriting. Other stops were made on the slow journey home: Spa, Maastricht, Louvain, Brussels and probably Antwerp (where they may have stayed near the cathedral and its 'steeple, in which there are said to be more than thirty bells') and towns in Holland.

On their return to England in September, Donne moved his family from the Isle of Wight and settled them, according to Walton, in 'a very convenient house rent-free' next to the Drury's place in Drury Lane, in a part of the street now covered by the south side of Aldwych. The rent is more likely to have been low than free, but it was in part of a pleasant mansion with gardens and courtyards and had to itself 'a little passage and a small court'. Some time after they moved, Donne's old friend Christopher Brooke became a neighbour and the couple's eighth child, Nicholas, was born.

On 6th November 1612, the heir to the throne, Prince Henry, died of typhoid, which inevitably postponed the celebration of the marriage of his sister the Princess Elizabeth to Frederick, the Elector Palatine. Donne published an ingenious but cold elegy on Henry, adding to the copious poetic output that greeted the prince's sudden death. A few months later, in February 1613, he wrote a more successful epithalamion in celebration of the royal marriage to add to the sumptuous festivities. This is the first verse:

An Epithalamion,
Or Marriage Song on the Lady *Elizabeth*
and *Count Palatine* being
Married on *St Valentines* Day

Haile Bishop Valentine, whose day this is,
  All the air is thy diocese,
  And all the chirping Choristers
And other birds are thy Parishioners,
  Thou marryest every yeare
The Lirique Lark, and the grave whispering Dove,
The Sparrow that neglects his life for love,
The household Bird, with the red stomacher,
  Thou mak'st the black bird speed as soone,
As doth the Goldfinch, or the Halcyon;
The husband cocke lookes out, and straight is sped,
And meets his wife, which brings her feather-bed.
This day more cheerfully than ever shine,
This day, which might enflame thy self, old Valentine

Not long after the wedding, Donne set off for Warwickshire to visit Sir Henry Goodyer at his estate at Polesworth, and from there made a visit to Sir Edward Herbert at Montgomery Castle, some sixty-five miles west of Polesworth. According to a manuscript enclosed with it, Donne sent back to Goodyer 'this meditation, on the way':

Good Friday, 1613. Riding Westward

LET mans Soule be a Spheare, and then, in this,
The intelligence that moves, devotion is,
And as the other Spheares, by being growne
Subject to forraigne motions, lose their owne,

And being by others hurried every day,
Scarce in a yeare their naturall forme obey:
Pleasure or business, so, our Soules admit
For their first mover, and are whirld by it.
Hence is't, that I am carryed towards the West
This day, when my Soules forme bends toward the East.
There I should see a Sunne, by rising set,
And by that setting endlesse day beget;
But that Christ on this Crosse, did rise and fall,
Sinne had eternally benighted all.
Yet dare I'almost be glad, I do not see
That spectacle of too much weight for mee.
Who sees Gods face, that is selfe life, must dye;
What a death were it then to see God dye?
It made his owne Lieutenant Nature shrinke,
It made his footstoole crack, and the Sunne winke.
Could I behold those hands which span the Poles,
And turne all spheares at once, peirc'd with those holes?
Could I behold that endlesse height which is
Zenith to us, and our Antipodes,
Humbled below us? or that blood which is
The seat of all our Soules, if not of his,
Made durt of dust, or that flesh which was worne
By God, for his apparell, rag'd, and torne?
If on these things I durst not looke, durst I
Upon his miserable mother cast mine eye,
Who was Gods partner here, and furnish'd thus
Halfe of that Sacrifice, which ransom'd us?
Though these things, as I ride, be from mine eye,
They'are present yet unto my memory,
For that looks towards them; and thou look'st towards mee,
O Saviour, as thou hang'st upon the tree;
I turne my backe to thee, but to receive
Corrections, till thy mercies bid thee leave.
O thinke mee worth thine anger, punish mee,

Burne off my rusts, and my deformity,
Restore thine Image, so much, by thy grace,
That thou may'st know mee, and I'll turne my face.

It was probably during this stay in the country that Donne reflected that the time might have come to find himself a different patron. Drury may have considered himself fit for high office, but he suffered from excessive self-esteem. A tactless inclination to speak his own mind was not likely to recommend him for a career in the diplomatic service, and since their return from the continent he had already been rebuked at court for complaining too noisily of the inadequate reception he felt he had received in Heidelberg. Donne set his sights instead on the rising star at Court, the King's favourite, Robert Ker, newly created Viscount Rochester and, after the King, the most powerful man in the land. Donne prevailed upon his old contact Lord Hay to recommend him to the odious Ker, which Hay duly did, first by presenting him with a letter from Donne and later by presenting him in person.

He may not have known how well-timed his representation was. Ker had recently lost the services of his talented factotum Sir Thomas Overbury, whom Ker himself had committed to the Tower on a trumped-up charge for opposing his intention to bring about a divorce between the Earl and Countess of Essex (with whom Ker was conducting an affair). Donne made a very favourable impression and from the evidence contained in his letters to Ker, it is clear that Donne was materially supported by him for about a year. In return, Donne offered to defend the divorce; the marriage was annulled, Ker and the Countess were married with the King's blessing in December 1613, and James promoted his favourite to the Earldom of Somerset so that his new wife's rank should be maintained. A couple of months later, their nuptials drew from Donne a further exercise in court flattery, another epithalamion, this time prefaced by an eclogue excusing its lateness:

Ecclogue
1613. December 26

*Allophanes finding Idios in the country in Christmas time,
reprehends his absence from court, at the marriage Of the Earle
of Sommerset; Idios gives his account of his purpose therein, and
of his absence thence.*

Allophanes
Unseasonable man, statue of ice,
   What could to countries solitude entice
Thee, in this yeares cold and decrepit time?
   Natures instinct drawes to the warmer clime
Even small birds, who by that courage dare,
   In numerous fleets, saile through their Sea, the aire.
What delicacie can in fields appeare,
   Whil'st Flora'herselfe doth a freeze jerkin weare?
Whil'st windes do all the trees and hedges strip
   Of leafes, to furnish roddes enough to whip
Thy madnesse from thee; and all springs by frost
   Have taken cold, and their sweet murmures lost;
If thou thy faults or fortunes would'st lament
   With just solemnity, do it in Lent;
At Court the spring already advanced is,
   The Sunne stayes longer up; and yet not his
The glory is, farre other, other fires...

Since Donne's return to London, a patron of longer standing,
Lady Bedford, had fallen gravely ill. On her recovery, which she
attributed in part to the attentions of the Puritan preacher John
Burgess, she was much changed. She shunned the court, and
when she did attend, according to the diarist John Chamberlain,
she was 'somewhat reformed in her attire, and forbears painting
[i.e. make-up], which they say makes her look somewhat

strangely'. Her spirits would not have been lifted by the loss of her brother in February 1614, a victim to smallpox. Donne, seeing an opportunity to work his way back into her favour, wrote a long and elaborate elegy in his memory. This passage begins at line 15:

Obsequies to the Lord Harrington,
brother the Lady Lucy, Countesse of Bedford

Thou seest mee here at midnight, now all rest;
Times dead-low water; when all mindes divest
To morrows businesse, when the labourers have
Such rest in bed, that their last Church-yard grave,
Subject to change, will scarce be'a type of this,
Now when the clyent, whose last hearing is
To morrow, sleeps, when the condemned man,
(Who when hee opes his eyes, must shut them then
Againe by death), although sad watch hee keepe,
Doth practice dying by a little sleepe,
Thou at this midnight seest mee, and as soone
As that Sunne rises to mee, midnight's noon,
All the world growes transparent, and I see
Through all, both Church and State, in seeing thee;
And I discerne by favour of this light,
My selfe, the hardest object of the sight.
God is the glasse; as thou when thou dost see
Him who sees all, seest all concerning thee,
So, yet unglorified, I comprehend
All, in these mirrors of thy wayes, and end...

Knowing that Lord Harrington's estate had passed to his sister, Donne somewhat tactlessly enclosed with the poem a begging letter. But if Donne's literary manoeuvres at this period often present him in a poor light, it should be borne in mind that 1613 and 1614 were years of sickness and misery. In September 1613 his eyesight seemed to be failing him and at Christmas he complained that the magnificent preparations being made for the Earl of Somerset's wedding might be, as far as he was concerned, in vain: 'It is one of my blind meditations to think what a miserable defeat it would be to all these preparations of bravery, if my infirmity should overtake others: for I am at least half blind, my windows are as full glasses as waters, as any mountebank's stall.' By February 1614, his eyesight had improved, but the rest of the family were sick and his wife had suffered a miscarriage. As he wrote to Goodyer:

> With me, Sir, it is thus. There is not one person (besides myself) in my house well. I have already lost half a child, and with that mischance of hers, my wife fallen into an indisposition, which would afflict her much, but the sickness of her children stupefies her; of one of which, in good faith, I have not much hope. This meets a fortune so ill provided for physic and such relief, that if God should ease us with burials, I know not well how to perform even that. I flatter myself in this, that I am dying too; nor can I truly die faster, by any waste, than by loss of children.

The family was indeed eased with burials, for the child of whom he had not much hope was probably his three-year-old daughter Mary, whose interment was registered at St Clement Danes on 18th May 1614 – at a cost of three shillings for the grave and two shillings and sixpence 'for the knell'.

The Rector of St Clement Danes, John Layfield, was one of a number of learned divines with whom Donne kept in touch in this period. He was also a regular at the Deanery of St Paul's and he often visited John King, the Bishop of London. Isaac Casaubon, the great French scholar, spent his last year on Drury Lane, very near where Donne lived, and it seems unlikely that he would not have come across him in 1613 or 1614. The Dutch jurist, Hugo Grotius, one of the intellectual heavyweights of the age, also visited London and moved in similar circles and Donne may have met him in 1613. There was no let-up in his own study of divinity and 'learned Languages', and the *Essays in Divinity* may well have been written, or at least completed, in these years. According to John Donne the younger, who published them in 1651 and wrote in the wisdom of hindsight, these represent 'the voluntary sacrifices of several hours, when he had many debates betwixt God and himself, whether he were worthy, and competently learned to enter Holy Orders'. Donne himself referred to them as sermons with 'no Auditory'.

In March 1614, Donne sought and was offered the seat of Taunton in advance of the so-called 'Addled Parliament' of April to June of that year. His appointment was in the gift of Sir Edward Phelips, the Master of the Rolls. The Addled Parliament is unusual in having passed no legislation at all and was entirely given over to questions of parliamentary privilege, members' grievances and efforts to remove monopolies. The King's Scottish favourites came in for a good deal of criticism, which put Donne in an awkward position, trapping him between Somerset, Ker and Hay on one side and Donne's sponsor Phelips, who was in favour of curbing royal prerogatives, on the other.

A few days after James impatiently dissolved parliament in June, four MPs were sent to the Tower for having been outspoken against the Scots. Characteristically, Donne seems not to have contributed to debates.

He had additional reason to keep quiet, since in the same month that he had been given a seat in Parliament, he had made a direct plea to Ker to get him the ambassadorship in Venice, an office now vacated by his old friend Sir Henry Wotton. His suit was probably not seriously considered, but after Parliament was dissolved he was in pursuit of Ker's support for another (unidentified) position. Any hopes for this were ruined by the unexpected arrival of the King of Denmark in London, which distracted the attention of the king and court. According to Walton, an appeal was made on Donne's behalf to the King later in 1614 with the backing of Ker, Hay and Donne's old boss Egerton, but in vain. He was once again advised to enter the Church.

This seems to have been Donne's last attempt to seek secular employment. By the end of November 1614, he had decided to bow to the will of the King and join the Church – a decision perhaps hastened by the death of his favourite son, Francis, who was buried, like his sister, at St Clement Danes on 10th November. He rode to Newmarket to tell James of his decision, and to exact from the King some assurance that he would, as he had previously promised, forward his career. At the same time, he cast about for ways of settling his debts before he took the momentous step. On learning of his intentions, Lady Bedford, touched by the 'Obsequies' Donne had written in memory of her brother, rashly offered to pay them all off. Unfortunately, her own financial situation proved not to be so flourishing, and Donne had to make do with only £30, with which he was bitterly disappointed. By calling upon 'more friends, then [sic.] I thought I should have needed', however, he succeeded in clearing his debts. Now that the die was cast, he also resolved to publish a collection of his poems 'as a valediction to the world, before I take Orders'. He called in manuscripts that he had sent to friends, making of himself 'a Rhapsoder of mine own rags, and that cost me more diligence, to seek them, then it did to make them'. But in the end, thinking perhaps that they might discredit the profession he was about to enter, he dropped the idea.

Ambassador to God:
The Priest

Donne was ordained Deacon and Priest in the chapel of the Bishop of London's palace on the north side of St Paul's on 23rd January 1615. In a rhapsodic passage, Walton maintained that, 'Now he had a new calling, new thoughts, and a new employment for his wit and eloquence: Now all his earthly affections were changed into divine love.' But the change was a good deal less dramatic than Walton suggests. Donne was not to put aside the arts of the courtier he had so assiduously, if not always successfully, practised in his previous life. Neither was he to forget the rather low opinion his peers generally entertained of an ecclesiastical career. A poem he wrote some four years later to another reluctant ordinand suggests some of the misgivings he felt about his action and the consciousness of diminished prestige:

To *Mr Tilman* after he had taken orders

Thou, whose diviner soule hath caus'd thee now
To put thy hand unto the holy Plough,
Making Lay-scornings of the Ministry,
Not an impediment, but victory;
What bringst thou home with thee? how is thy mind
Affected in the vintage? Doest thou finde

New thoughts and stirrings in thee? and as Steele
Toucht with a Loadstone, dost new motions feele?
Or, as a Ship after much paine and care,
For Iron and Cloth brings home rich Indian ware,
Hast thou thus traffiqu'd, but with farre more gaine
Of noble goods, and with lesse time and paine?
Thou art the same materials, as before,
Onely the stamp is changed; but no more?
And as new crowned Kings alter the face,
But not the monies substance; so hath grace
Chang'd onely Gods old Image by Creation,
To Christs new stamp, at this thy Coronation;
Or, as we paint Angels with wings, because
They beare Gods message, and proclaime his lawes,
Since thou must doe the like, and so must move,
Art thou new feather'd with celestiall love?
Deare, tell me where thy purchase lies, and shew
What thy advantage is above, below.
But if thy gainings do surmount expression,
Why doth the foolish world scorne that profession,
Whose joys passe speech? Why do they think unfit
That Gentry should joyne families with it?
As if their day were onely to be spent
In dressing, Mistressing and complement;
Alas poore joyes, but poorer men, whose trust
Seems richly placed in sublimed dust;
(For, such are cloathes and beauty, which though gay,
Are, at the best, but as sublimed clay.)
Let then the world thy calling disrespect,
But goe thou on, and pitty their neglect.
What function is so noble, as to bee
Embassador to God and destinie?
To open life, to give kingdomes to more
Than Kings give dignities; to keepe heavens doore?
Maries prerogative was to beare Christ, so

'Tis preachers to convey him, for they doe
As Angels out of clouds, from Pulpits speake;
And bless the poor beneath, the lame, the weake.
If then th'Astronomers, whereas they spie
A new-found Starre, their Opticks magnifie,
How brave are those, who with their Engine, can
Bring man to heaven, and heaven againe to man?
These are thy titles and preheminences,
In whom must meet Gods graces, mens offences,
And so the heavens which beget all things here,
And the earth our mother, which these things doth beare
Both these in thee, are in thy Calling knit,
And make thee now a blest Hermaphrodite.

To mark the change in his life, Donne commissioned a new seal, showing the device of Christ crucified on an anchor, and wrote punningly to George Herbert of 'Our old coat lost, unto new arms I go.' He once again visited James at Newmarket to present himself as a priest and was soon afterwards (the date is unknown) made one of forty-eight Chaplains-in-Ordinary to the King. This was a desirable position, since royal chaplains, as well as enjoying access to the Court, were granted two additional benefices, which brought a comparatively high income. In March, the King requested Donne to accompany him on an official visit to Cambridge University, where, after the disputations, plays and feasts were concluded, a number of honorary degrees were given out. The university put up considerable resistance against granting a degree to Donne, and it was only when a royal mandate was delivered after the King's departure that a doctorate was conferred upon him. As the diarist John Chamberlain wrote, 'John Dun and one Cheeke went out doctors at Cambridge with much ado after our coming away, by the King's express mandate, though the vice chancellor and some other of the heads called them openly *filios noctis et tenebriones* [sons of night and shadows] that sought thus to come in at the window, when there was a fair gate open.' The newly ordained Donne seems at first to have been regarded with suspicion not just in the university but throughout the Church.

He remained with his family at Drury Lane, but without Sir Robert, who died on his estate at Hawstead shortly after Donne's return from Cambridge. He began his preaching career in a modest way, learning his craft at parish churches and chapels in Paddington, Greenwich, and, especially, Camberwell. His learning and literary ability were not in question, but he needed to work at his delivery and manner. By and large, these sermons stick to the interpretation of scripture rather than offering advice to his congregation. His first surviving court sermon, preached at Whitehall on 21st April 1616 (two days before Shakespeare's death) was one of many preached before the King in subsequent Aprils and during Lent.

A month later, Donne had occasion to feel greatly comforted at his new choice of career. On 24th May 1616 the Countess of Somerset pleaded guilty to the murder of Sir Thomas Overbury and the Earl, Donne's old patron, was found guilty the next day. It transpired that during Overbury's wholly undeserved imprisonment in the Tower, they had plotted with the staff, in the manner of a Jacobean tragedy, to feed him poisoned tarts and jellies. The Somersets remained in the Tower, overseen by its recently appointed Lieutenant, Sir George More, for five years. It must have been a relief to Donne that, although he had been Somerset's dependant while the murder was committed, he was no longer closely attached to him.

His daughter Margaret was born in April, and about this time his sister, Anne, died, which drew from Donne a moving letter to his mother, whose life he describes as 'a sea, under a continual tempest, where one wave hath ever overtaken another'. He was now the last of her children alive and it seems they had seen little of each other in recent years. He begged to be forgiven his 'negligences' and swore to be more attentive in future: 'For my part, which am only left now, to do the office of a child; though the poorness of my fortune, and the greatness of my charge, hath not suffered me to express my duty towards you, as became me; yet, I protest to you before Almighty God, and his Angels and Saints in Heaven, that I do, and ever shall, esteem myself, to be as strongly bound to look to you, and provide for your relief, as for my own poor wife and children.' This promise he fulfilled under what must have been difficult circumstances for an ambitious priest in the Church of England, since his mother remained a Roman Catholic. She, in turn, cannot have looked kindly on her son's ordination or his attacks in print on the Jesuits.

Meanwhile, Donne took full advantage of the pluralistic privileges that came with his royal chaplaincy. A year after his ordination he received the benefices of Keyston in Huntingdonshire (from the King) and Sevenoaks in Kent (from Egerton, his old master, now Lord Chancellor), but on condition that he need not be resident in either. Occasional preaching visits aside, the congregation was left to the care of a curate or resident vicar. In October, his growing talent for preaching secured him the appointment of Reader (or Preacher) at Lincoln's Inn, which required that he deliver about fifty sermons a year, but demanded little in the way of pastoral care and gave him an annual salary of £60. Moreover, 'the love of that noble society was expressed to him many ways' and 'fair lodgings... were set apart and newly furnished for him, with all necessaries.' Lincoln's Inn was, moreover, only a short walk from Drury Lane. Its congregation was learned and professional; he knew many of the auditors and they knew him and he was able to inject personal reminiscence and wit into his preaching. He learned the skill of tailoring his style to his congregation. The sermons at Lincoln's Inn are filled with legal images, the sermons at Whitehall with the language of the Court.

In August 1617, after a week spent preaching in Sevenoaks, Donne returned to London to find his wife had given birth to a still-born child – and on 15th August, at the age of only thirty-three, Ann Donne died. Mother and child were buried the next day in St Clement Danes, in the church where two other of the couple's children already lay. Donne commissioned a monument to her from the sculptor Nicholas Stone (the draft inscription he sent to his father-in-law survives). What can be said about her? She may or may not have been the object of much of his greatest poetry. No image of her survives and, in spite of Donne's large correspondence, there is little or no record of her character. She had been 'transplanted into a wretched fortune' and she had borne her husband twelve children, and lost five. He promised those that remained that they would not come under the 'subjection of a step-mother'. And if Ann is really the absent woman in what is arguably the greatest of the *Songs and Sonnets*, then no other could take her place anyway.

A nocturnall upon S. *Lucies* day, Being the shortest day

Tis the yeares midnight, and it is the dayes,
Lucies, who scarce seaven houres herself unmaskes,
*   The Sunne is spent, and now his flasks*
*   Send forth light squibs, no constant rayes;*
*   The worlds whole sap is sunke:*
The generall balme th'hydroptique earth hath drunk,
Whither, as to the beds-feet, life is shrunke,
Dead and enterr'd; yet all these seeme to laugh,
Compar'd with mee, who am their Epitaph.

Study me then, you who shall lovers bee
At the next world, that is, at the next Spring:
*   For I am every dead thing,*
*   In whom love wrought new Alchimie.*
*   For his art did expresse*

A quintessence even from nothingnesse,
From dull privations, and leane emptinesse:
He ruin'd mee, and I am re-begot
Of absence, darknesse, death; things which are not.

All others, from all things, draw all that's good,
Life, soule, forme, spirit, whence they beeing have;
    I, by loves limbecke, am the grave
    Of all, that's nothing. Oft a flood
        Have wee two wept, and so
Drownd the whole world, us two; oft did we grow
To be two Chaosses, when we did show
Care to ought else; and often absences
Withdrew our soules, and made us carcasses.

But I am by her death, (which word wrongs her)
Of the first nothing, the Elixer grown;
    Were I a man, that I were one,
    I needs must know; I should preferre,
        If I were any beast,
Some ends, some means; Yea plants, yea stones detest,
And love; All, all some properties invest;
If I an ordinary nothing were,
As shadow, a light, and body must be here.

But I am None; nor will my Sunne renew.
You lovers, for whose sake, the lesser Sunne
    At this time to the Goat is runne
    To fetch new lust, and give it you,
        Enjoy your summer all;
Since shee enjoyes her long nights festivall,
Let mee prepare towards her, and let mee call
This houre her Vigill, and her Eve, since this
Both the yeares, and the dayes deep midnight is.

And so, as Walton writes, 'his very soul was elemented of nothing but sadness' and 'he began the day and ended the night; ended the restless night and began the weary day in lamentations.' He emerged from his grieving solitude to deliver Ann's funeral sermon to the congregation at St Clement Danes, where, Walton continues, he 'melted and moulded them into a companionable sadness; and so they left the Congregation; but then their houses presented them with objects of diversion: and his, presented him with nothing but fresh objects of sorrow, in beholding many helpless children, a narrow fortune, and a consideration of the many cares and casualties that attend their education.' After Ann's death a deeper religious feeling enters into the sermons and divine poems. As 'Holy Sonnet 17' reveals, it served to concentrate his religious vocation and to bring him closer to an understanding and feeling for the positive aspects of his faith:

> *Since she whom I lov'd hath payd her last debt*
> *To Nature, and to hers, and my good is dead,*
> *And her Soule early into heaven ravished,*
> *Wholly on heavenly things my mind is sett.*
> *Here the admyring her my mind did whett*
> *To seeke thee God; so streames do shew their head,*
> *But though I have found thee, and thou my thirst hast fed,*
> *A holy thirsty dropsy melts mee yett.*
> *But why should I begg more Love, when as thou*
> *Dost wooe my soule for hers; offring all thine:*
> *And dost not only feare lest I allow*
> *My Love to Saints and Angels, things divine,*
> *But in thy tender jealousy dost doubt*
> *Lest the World, Fleshe, yea Devill put thee out.*

The possibility of a grieving retirement was put out of the question eighteen months later when, in 1619, Donne was persuaded to serve as chaplain to James Hay, now Viscount

Doncaster, on a diplomatic mission to Germany and the Low Countries. Its origins lay in James' ambition to broker a peace between the Bohemian Protestants (led by his son-in-law Frederick) and the Holy Roman Emperor and prevent the escalation of a larger conflict. Donne was probably chosen because of his insight into religious controversy and because of his brilliance as a preacher. A cipher given to Donne in 1615 (and preserved in the Public Record Office) for use in diplomatic correspondence also suggests that he had been in touch with leading religious figures and perhaps agents for the previous four years. From a personal point of view, however, the offer came too late. After the strenuous attempts he had made as a layman at getting a diplomatic position, Donne now embraced his commission without enthusiasm. 'I leave,' he wrote to Goodyer, 'a scattered flock of wretched children, and I carry an infirm and valetudinary body, and I go into the mouth of such adversaries, as I cannot blame for hating me, the Jesuits, and yet I go.' Although he would be travelling in comfort, even luxury, with a large embassy, he feared that he would never return. But if he did, he hoped the journey would put a 'sea' between himself and the faults of his past.

A Hymne to Christ, at the
Authors last going into Germany

IN what torne ship soever I embarke,
That ship shall be my embleme of thy Arke;
What sea soever swallow mee, that flood
Shall be to mee an embleme of thy blood;
Though thou with clouds of anger do disguise
Thy face; yet through that maske I know those eyes,
    Which, though they turne away sometimes,
      They never will despise.

I sacrifice this Iland unto thee,
And all whom I lov'd there, and who lov'd mee;
When I have put our seas twixt them and mee,
Put thou thy sea betwixt my sinnes and thee.
As the trees sap doth seeke the root below
In winter, in my winter now I goe,
*   Where none but thee, th'Eternall root*
*   Of true Love I may know.*

Nor thou nor thy religion dost controule,
The amorousnesse of an harmonious Soule,
But thou would'st have that love thy selfe: As thou
Art jealous, Lord, so I am jealous now,
Thou lov'st not, till from loving more, thou free
My soule: Who ever gives, takes libertie:
*   O, if thou car'st not whom I love*
*   Alas, thou lov'st not mee.*

Seale then this bill of my Divorce to All,
On whom those fainter beames of love did fall;
Marry those loves, which in youth scattered bee
On Fame, Wit, Hopes (false mistresses) to thee.
Churches are best for Prayer, that have least light:
To see God only, I goe out of sight:
*   And to scape stormy dayes, I chuse*
*   An Everlasting night*

The embassy travelled via Calais and Antwerp to Mariemont (where it met the Archduke) and thence to Heidelberg to see Frederick, the Elector Palatine and Princess Elizabeth, where Donne preached a sermon. It then proceeded to Ulm, Augsburg and Munich for parleys with allies of the Emperor. Doncaster met Frederick at Salzburg and tried to make the case for the Bohemian Protestants, but his efforts were unavailing. At the imperial elections at Frankfurt it became plain that diplomatic intervention was having no effect and the embassy moved on to Spa. Frederick was made King of Bohemia and Ferdinand, Emperor. The embassy followed the new emperor to Graz, but Doncaster failed to persuade Ferdinand to follow a peaceful course. They set off on the long journey home, stopping off at The Hague, where Donne preached and was presented with a medal struck in commemoration of the Synod of Dort – a gift that shows he was recognised as a moderate and sympathetic European Protestant. The delegation reached London in January 1620, having done nothing to prevent what was to become the Thirty Years' War. It was probably around this time that he wrote 'Holy Sonnet 18', a subtly questioning poem that probes the question: which is the best and truest church?

> Show me deare Christ, thy spouse, so bright and clear.
> What! is it She, which on the other shore
> Goes richly painted? or which rob'd and tore
> Laments and mournes in Germany and here?
> Sleepes she a thousand, then peepes up one yeare?
> Is she selfe truth and errs? now new, now outwore?
> Doth she, and did she, and shall she evermore
> On one, on seven, or on no hill appeare?
> Dwells she with us, or like adventuring knights
> First travaile we to seek and then make Love?
> Betray kind husband thy spouse to our sights,
> And let myne amorous soule court thy mild Dove,
> Who is most trew, and most pleasing to thee, then
> When she'is embrac'd and open to most men.

Donne returned to his duties at Lincoln's Inn, with, according to Walton, 'his sorrows moderated, and his health improved; and there betook himself to his constant course of Preaching'. At the same time he kept himself before those in power, not least the King's current favourite, the loathsome George Villiers,

Duke of Buckingham, who now possessed a near monopoly on royal patronage. Donne declared to him that, 'I lie in a corner, as a clod of clay, attending what kind of vessel' it would please the Duke to make of him. By such courtly prostrations, he was most likely to secure a deanery when a vacancy might arise. It was the kind of language Villiers liked. Eventually, after several disappointments, such a vacancy presented itself on 26th August 1621, with the death of the Bishop of Exeter. Valentine Cary, Dean of St Paul's, was chosen to succeed him, leaving the deanery vacant. If Walton is to be believed (which in this case is doubtful), the King summoned Donne and declared that, 'I have invited you to Dinner; and, though you sit not down with me, yet I will carve to you of a dish that I know you love well; for knowing you love London, I do therefore make you Dean of Pauls; and when I have dined, then do you take your beloved dish home to your study; say grace to yourself, and much good may it do you.'

A part of the main:
The Dean

He gave up his living at Keyston and resigned from Lincoln's Inn, leaving as a parting gift a deluxe six-volume edition of the Bible. As Dean, he would be responsible for the administration of the cathedral and its properties and estates. The records (or act books) during his period of office have not survived, but what evidence there is suggests that he was efficient and conscientious, but not a zealous reformer of existing practices. He seems to have done little or nothing to improve, for instance, the conduct of the general public in St Paul's (which had for years used the building as a thoroughfare and general meeting place) or to repair the crumbling fabric of the huge ancient cathedral, apparently turning a blind eye when a large concession of Portland stone bought for repairs was appropriated by the Duke of Buckingham for the rebuilding of York House, now the favourite's palace on the Strand. It has been suggested that this was an indirect bribe Donne 'paid' to Villiers for his deanery. Some of the stone probably survives in the water gate at Victoria Gardens, the only relic that survives of the old palace.

He was not required to give sermons in the cathedral more than a few times a year (at Christmas, Easter and on Ascension day), but he chose to preach more often, as well as at Chiswick (where, as Dean, he was prebend), and at his country parishes in the summer. After he became Dean, a stronger note of ecclesiastical authority entered his sermons where necessary.

At those he delivered at the great outdoor pulpits at St Paul's Cross and St Mary Spital, such as one given in support of James' unpopular 'Directions to Preachers' (which, amongst other things, sought to rule that only senior members of the Church might preach on the subject of predestination), he was effectively an official spokesman for the King. In response to the miscellaneous congregations they needed to appeal to, the sermons at St Paul's were more direct in tone. They were also highly emotional, even theatrical, performances. He was, describes Walton:

> ... a Preacher in earnest; weeping sometimes for his Auditory, sometimes with them; always preaching to himself, like an Angel from a cloud, but in none; carrying some, as St Paul was, to heaven in holy raptures, and enticing others by a sacred Art and Courtship to amend their lives; here picturing a vice so as to make it ugly to those that practised it; and a virtue so as to make it be beloved even by those that lov'd it not; and all this with a most particular grace and an unexpressible addition of comeliness.

In 1622 he was granted the rectory of Blunham in Bedfordshire by the Earl of Kent, and in the same year he was made a Justice of the Peace for Kent and Bedfordshire. Other official positions followed. He joined the board of the Company of the Virginia Plantation, heard appeals in the lower ecclesiastical courts, sat in the Court of Delegates and on the Court of High Commission, which inquired into ecclesiastical abuses, and in 1626 was made a governor of the Charterhouse, recently converted into a school and hospital. His legal knowledge was kept in good use and he remained a sort of honorary bencher of Lincoln's Inn and returned there in 1623 to preach a dedicatory sermon for the new chapel. His association with the legal profession was reinforced in March 1624, when the Earl of Dorset (in whose gift it was) granted him the parish of St Dunstan-in-the-West, in the midst of legal London. As a lifelong bookworm, he must also have been pleased to live and work at the heart of the publishing trade, since most of the city's booksellers and stationers were based in the churchyards of St Dunstan's and St Paul's.

He remained in favour with the King and Buckingham, receiving from his various livings an income of approximately £2,000 (out of which he dispensed charity, paid his curates and other expenses including the hospitality he was expected to provide as Dean). And he was comfortably accommodated at the Deanery, a handsome and substantial old house south-west of the cathedral with a large household, including his mother and children and a number of servants. One child was the nineteen-year-old Constance, who divided her time between here and the family of Donne's sister-in-law in Peckham. It was probably through this family (the Grymeses) that in October 1623 Donne came to know or became reacquainted with the great actor and benefactor, Edward Alleyn, now well established on his estate in Dulwich. On the 21st, he sat down with Alleyn and his brother-in-law and discussed terms for the marriage of Constance to the much older Alleyn. The 'strangest match' was made and the couple, their wedding hastened by Donne's illness, were married within six weeks. The relationship between Donne and his elderly son-in-law later cooled and two years later was soured by a quarrel over a reluctance on both sides (but chiefly Donne's) to meet the financial obligations they had agreed to. Beyond this difference there is a mean-spirited aspect to Donne's dealings with Alleyn that suggests he was uncomfortable about the match. Fortunately, matters were patched up before Alleyn's death in 1626.

The illness that had encouraged Donne to precipitate Constance's marriage was relapsing fever, which in the winter of 1623 raged in the city, and which, in spite of bringing insomnia and weakness, is unusual in leaving the patient mentally alert. Donne's own physician, Dr Fox, attended him, as did the King's, who placed dead pigeons at his feet 'to draw the vapours from the head'. During this fever, which nearly cost him his life, Donne scribbled down (or at least conceived) the reflections that form the basis of his *Devotions*. The worst stages of his illness coincided with the height of the epidemic itself, when the bells of St Gregory by Pauls, in common with many other parish churches, tolled for those who had died:

> No man is an island, entire of itself; every man is a piece of the continent, a part of the main; if a clod be washed away by the sea, Europe is the less, as well as if a promontory were, as well as if a manor of thy friend's or thy friends or of thine own were; any man's death diminishes me, because I am involved in mankind; and therefore never send to know for whom the bell tolls; it tolls for thee.

He passed the dangerous stage; no fatal relapse came and in the period of his convalescence he worked up the notes he had made during his illness into the *Devotions*, which were published only a few weeks after he first fell ill. The book is composed of twenty-three numbered parts, each one corresponding to a 'station' of the disease, and divided in turn into a meditation on the human condition, an expostulation (or 'debatement' with God) and a prayer. They are the best introduction to his religious prose, bringing out, as the scholar Douglas Bush has written 'all Donne's special characteristics, his preoccupation with sin and death, his acuteness of psychological analysis, his keen awareness of the tension between his soul and the world, the originality of his wit, the troubled and sometimes lurid power of his imagination'. At around the same time, he also wrote the 'Hymn to God my God, in my Sickness' and 'A Hymn to God the Father'. The latter, according to Walton, Donne arranged 'to be set to a most grave and solemn tune' and sung at St Paul's especially during the evening service:

A Hymne to God the Father

I

Wilt thou forgive that sinne where I begunne,
Which was my sin, though it were done before?
Wilt thou forgive that sinne; through which I runne,
And do run still: though still I do deplore?
When thou hast done, thou hast not done,
For, I have more.

II

Wilt thou forgive that sinne by which I have wonne
Others to sin? and, made my sin their doore?
Wilt thou forgive that sinne which I did shunne
A yeare, or two: but wallowed in, a score?
When thou hast done, thou hast not done,
For I have more.

III

I have a sinne of feare, that when I have spunne
My last thread, I shall perish on the shore;
But sweare by thy selfe, that at my death thy sonne
Shall shine as it shines now, and heretofore;
And, having done that, Thou hast done,
I feare no more.

In March 1625, King James died, and in the memorial sermon Donne preached for him at Denmark House, the late Queen's residence, he touched upon the passing of the old dispensation, and a 'going forth in many several ways: some to the service of their new master, and some to their enjoying of their fortunes conferred by their old; some to the raising of new hopes, some to the burying of old'. Donne was also the first to preach (somewhat nervously) to Charles I when he came out of mourning and, aside from one occasion two years later when he gave unintentional offence to the new King in a Lent sermon, he weathered the transition well. With the rise of William Laud (who became Donne's bishop in 1628) and his brand of high Anglicanism, there followed a change of focus in Donne's preaching. Rome is criticised less than the rising Puritanism, and in a sermon delivered at Paul's Cross in 1627 he defended church ritual and religious adornment and expressed a wish that he made many times throughout his career as a divine: the establishment of a united, truly Catholic church, 'one flock, in one fold, under one Shepherd, though not all of one colour, of one practice in all outward and disciplinarian points.'

Later in 1625 he was ill again, this time with a bronchial infection, and retired with his family to the house in Chelsea belonging to his old friend Magdalen Herbert, now Lady Danvers, who some years previously had married Sir John Danvers. His recuperation there coincided with an outbreak of plague in the city, which lengthened his stay to six months. In the lovely Italianate garden at the Danvers' large house near the river, he transcribed and improved his sermons and deepened his acquaintance with George Herbert, who was also staying there for a time and on the brink of taking holy orders. He was impressed by the charity towards the sick that Magdalen Danvers showed when the plague 'fell hotly' on Chelsea. The extraordinary sermon he preached at St Dunstan's in December, after it had abated, is filled with references to the city's late ordeal, where 'every grain of dust that flies here, is a piece of a Christian'.

The following year, the deaths that touched Donne were those of people far closer to him. His daughter Lucy, Sir Henry Goodyer, Lady Bedford and Lady Danvers herself all died within the space of a few months; and in February 1628, he lost Christopher Brooke. He also made new and developed old friendships. George Garrard, with whom he had lodged at the Savoy years before, and Ann Cokayne, a neighbour of Goodyer's, feature regularly amongst the recipients of Donne's letters towards the end of his life. Izaak Walton's record of his presence at the startling sermon Donne preached at the memorial service for Lady Danvers at Chelsea is the first indication that Donne and his first biographer were acquainted.

Alleyn's death in November 1626 had left Constance free to remarry, and in June 1630 her wedding to Sir James Harvey was celebrated in Camberwell. It was during a visit to the married couple with his mother (now in her late eighties) at their house at Aldborough Hatch in Essex, that Donne fell ill again, but with more than one of those fevers with which he by now paid every half-year 'as a rent for my life'. He used the months he spent resting there working up his sermons from notes as he had done in Chelsea; but this time there was to be no recuperation. In December, at the age of fifty-eight, he made his will, leaving an estate to his children of between £3,000 and £4,000, numerous legacies to servants, money to the poor of the parish and specific gifts to his remaining friends, including the striking portrait of himself 'taken in shadows' now in the National Portrait Gallery. He made no provision for his poems, long since scattered among friends. A few weeks later, in January, his mother died.

Donne had expressed the wish that he 'might die in the Pulpit', and it is his mother's death as well as his own that pervades 'Death's Duel', his last and most theatrical sermon, which he preached before Charles I on 25th February 1631. He was by then half wasted away, and many of those who saw him felt, in Walton's words, that, 'he presented himself not to preach mortification by a living voice; but, mortality by a decayed body and a dying face,' and that, 'Dr Donne had preach'd his own funeral sermon.'

After this final public appearance and a meeting of the governors of the Charterhouse the following day, Donne withdrew from the world. But he had one last task to perform. He commissioned a wooden urn to be carved and ordered a wooden board the length of his body to be brought. An artist was sent for, and, when charcoal fires had been lit in his study, he undressed and wrapped himself in his shroud, fastening it with knots at top and bottom, leaving only his face exposed. With his eyes shut and his emaciated face turned towards the east, he stood on the urn for his full-length portrait to be made. The finished drawing presented his image at the moment of resurrection, slowly rising from his funeral urn.

Having taken leave of his friends, and with the drawing at his bedside, he lay for some ten days waiting for his end. At last, on 31st March 1631, as Walton writes, 'his last breath departed from him, he closed his own eyes; and then disposed his hands and body into such a posture as required not the least alteration by those that came to shroud him.'

A mine of rich and pregnant fancy:
Afterlife

The drawing Donne had kept beside his bed became the model for the engraving Martin Droeshout cut for the frontispiece to 'Death's Duel', his final sermon. The gaunt and wasted face it shows suggest a more faithful rendering of the original than the comparatively serene monument Nicholas Stone carved to stand above Donne's resting place in St Paul's – one of the very few artefacts from the old cathedral to survive the Great Fire.

Donne's poems, as has been repeated here, were not well known in his lifetime, and circulated only quite slowly, passing from one manuscript collection to another. Things changed quite rapidly after his death. In 1633 the first collection of his *Poems* appeared (reprinted only two years later and another five times over the following twenty years) with contributions from, among others, John Marston, Ben Jonson, Izaak Walton and Thomas Carew, praising Donne in more or less equal measure as poet, scholar and divine. The publisher (echoing Jonson's earlier praise of the elegies...?), no doubt with the readers of manuscript collections in mind, confidently asserted that they were'the best judgements... the best in this kind, that ever this kingdom hath yet seen.' Of the elegies that prefaced the collection, Carew's is the best and remains the best known:

Thou hast redeem'd, and opened us a mine
Of rich and pregnant fancy, drawn a line
Of masculine expression...

Carew was one of a number of mid-17th-century poets (a company that includes George Herbert, Richard Crashaw, Henry Vaughan and, later, Andrew Marvell) who found in Donne's poetry the model of a new literary style.

The early editions of Donne's poems contained some of his letters (eleven in the 1633 edition) and his son, though a careless, even reckless editor, determined to cash in on his father's ecclesiastical celebrity and published his father's *Letters to Severall Persons of Honour* in 1651, and the remainder ten years later. In all, 150 of Donne's letters were published within thirty years of his death, far more than any of his literary contemporaries. Donne was also, of course, the subject of a biography (or hagiography) by Walton, written only nine years after his death (though revised and expanded over thirty-five years). Walton's chronology is often inaccurate, he conflates his sources, and he is more interested in and sympathetic to the Dean of St Paul's than the poet, soldier and courtier, but he had known his subject and many of his friends, and he caught the main outlines of Donne's life preserving it in a minor classic of English prose.

In the Restoration, Donne's reputation suffered a reversal. In the smoother age of Dryden, his metres were considered rough and his conceits overpowering and distracting. Dryden himself censured Donne for elevating wit above feeling: 'He affects the metaphysics, not only in his satires, but in his amorous verses, where Nature only should reign; and perplexes the minds of the fair sex with nice speculations of philosophy, when he should engage their hearts, and entertain them with the softnesses of love.' His views were taken up by his literary successors. The Satires were only fit to be read if they were given an Augustan polish, which is what Pope gave Satires 2 and 4. But it was Johnson, in his 'Life of Cowley', who attacked Donne and his successors with the greatest vigour. He saw Donne's poems as roughly worked tissues of conceits, not arguments, in which 'the most heterogeneous ideas are yoked by violence together'. Moreover, they were indecent. Critical damnation and literary prejudice were reinforced by half-knowledge as old editions of the poems became hard to find and new versions were inaccurate and poorly edited.

Donne's rehabilitation began with the Romantics. Hazlitt, following Johnson, found him repulsive, irrelevantly recondite and self-centred, but his contemporaries thought otherwise. Charles Lamb discovered in Donne a 'warmth of soul and gener-ous feeling'; De Quincey found 'a diamond dust of rhetorical brilliances' strewed over all the verse and prose and even admired the much-maligned 'Metempsychosis'. But it was Coleridge who read him most attentively and sympathetically, finding not, as Johnson had, rhapsodies, but arguments; and instead of coldness and eccentricity, a powerful and distinctive poetic voice. In 'On Donne's Poetry' (1818), he writes:

I

With Donne, whose muse on dromedary trots,
Wreathe iron pokers into true-love knots;
Rhyme's sturdy cripple, fancy's maze and clue,
Wit's forge and fire-blast, meaning's press and screw.

Even his faults were representative of his age:

II

See lewdness and theology combined –
A cynic and a sycophantic mind;
A fancy shared party per pale between
Death's head and skeletons and Aretine! –
Not his peculiar defect or crime,
But the true current mintage of the time.

Such were the establish'd signs and tokens given
To mark a loyal churchman, sound and even,
Free from papistic and fanatic leaven.

Among the Victorians, it was Robert Browning who most admired the 'revered and magisterial Donne'. In 'The Two Poets of Croisic', he quotes Donne's 'Metempsychosis' and makes a character say of him: 'Better and truer verse none ever wrote.' His dramatic monologues owe much to Donne, and Donne's example encouraged Browning to reintroduce difficulty, colloquialism and awkward metre back into English poetry.

Browning may have taken the quotation from 'Metempsychosis' from Alexander Grosart's first modern edition of the poems, published some six years before, in 1872. The great strides in Donne scholarship, however, were taken at the turn of the century with, for instance, E.K. Chambers' edition of the poems, which appeared in 1896 with an introduction by George Saintsbury, and in 1899 the publication of the *Life and Letters of John Donne* by Sir Edmund Gosse (now best known for his great autobiography, *Father and Son*), which revealed that Donne was the earliest English poet of whom anything resembling a personal biography could be written.

Chambers' edition was surpassed in 1912 by a pioneering two-volume collection of the poems edited by Herbert Grierson, which remains the starting point for most modern scholarly editions. It was T.S. Eliot's review of an associated work by Grierson (*Metaphysical Poetry: Donne to Butler*, 1921) that established Donne as a proto-modernist, even if the poet Eliot described sounds less like John Donne than T.S. Eliot:

A thought to Donne was an experience; it modified his sensibility. When a poet's mind is perfectly equipped for its work, it is constantly amalgamating disparate experience; the ordinary man's experience is chaotic, irregular, fragmentary. The latter falls in love, or reads Spinoza, and these two experiences have nothing to do with each other, or with the noise of the typewriter or the smell of cooking; in the mind of the poet these experiences are always forming new wholes.

It only took the approbation of three of Eliot's most influential followers, I.A. Richards, F.R. Leavis and William Empson to push Donne into the heart of the university English curriculum. In some measure, his 'difficulty' may even have boosted the academic status of English itself. Reading him demands obvious effort. Since then, critical and scholarly attention has been mountainous. Two major figures in the second half of the twentieth century included Dame Helen Gardner, who, in 1952 produced an important edition of the religious poems (significantly, she was also an expert on Eliot), and R.C. Bald, whose outstanding *John Donne: A Life* (1970), is unlikely to be surpassed (even by John Stubbs' vivid 2006 biography, *Donne: The Reformed Soul*). Bald's biography provided the chief source for this book. It also furnished the biographical information in John Carey's *John Donne: Life, Mind and Art* (1981), which remains the most penetrating and entertaining study of Donne's imagination.

Donne's tenth Holy Sonnet (the fourteenth in Grierson's edition) 'Batter my heart three-personed God' is sung at the climax of John Adams' *Doctor Atomic*, his 2005 opera about 'Trinity', the first test of the atomic bomb at Los Alamos in 1945 and its mastermind, the nuclear physicist J. Robert Oppenheimer, one of Donne's most surprising admirers. And in 2008, a new two-volume annotated edition of the poems edited by Robin Robbins appeared. Interest in Donne shows no sign of abating.

List of Works

Unfortunately many of Donne's poems cannot be dated with much accuracy and many can hardly be dated at all. All that can be said about the dating of most of the *Songs and Sonnets* is that there is no positive evidence for their having been written before 1602. Which doesn't mean they were not.

Where it was possible to introduce the poems chronologically, I have usually done so. Elsewhere, I have chosen to introduce them where they seemed to shed light on some aspect of the life and vice versa.

pp. 9–10: 'The Relique' (unknown; after 1602?)
pp. 10–12: from *Pseudo-Martyr* (1609)
p. 16: 'The Flea' (unknown; after 1602?)
pp. 21–4: 'Satyre I' (c.1593)
p. 25: 'To Mr E.G.' (1593)
pp. 28–31: 'Satyre III' (1594/5)
pp. 31–3: 'Elegie IV: The Perfume' (1593–6)
pp. 36–7: 'The Curse' (unknown; after 1602?)
pp. 38–9: 'Elegy XVI: On his Mistris' (1599–1601?)
p. 41: 'A Burnt Ship' (1596)
pp. 42–4: 'The Storme' (1597)
pp. 45–6: 'The Calme' (1598)
p. 49: from 'Satyre V' (1598?)
p. 51: 'The good-morrow' (unknown; after 1602?)
p. 53: 'The Expiration' (before 1609)
p. 55: 'The Anniversarie' (not before 1603?)
pp. 56–7: 'Elegy IX: The Autumnall' (1600?)
pp. 58–60: from 'The Progresse of the Soule: Metempsychosis' (1601)
pp. 64–5: 'The Canonization' (unknown; after 1602?)
pp. 66–7: 'Elegy XIX: Going to Bed' (1593–6?; c.1602?)
p. 68: from 'To Sir Henry Wotton at His Going Ambassador
    to Venice' (1604)
p. 69: 'The Sunne Rising' (not before 1603?)
pp. 73–5: 'To Sir Henry Goodyere' (1608?)
p. 76: 'Aire and Angels' (unknown; after 1602?)
pp. 77–8: 'Twicknam Garden' (unknown; 1607 or later)
p. 79: 'The Funerall' (unknown; after 1602?)
p. 80: 'La Corona' (c.1609)
pp. 81–3: 'The Exstasie' (unknown; after 1602?)
p. 86: from *Pseudo-Martyr* (1609)
p. 87: from *St Ignatius his Conclave* (1610)
p. 89: from *Biathanatos* (c.1607–8)

Further Reading

Quotations from Donne's poetry in this book are taken from *Donne: Poetical Works*, ed. Herbert J.C. Grierson, 1929. Reprinted by kind permission of the Herbert Grierson estate.

Donne's Poetry and Prose
Devotions upon Emergent Occasions, Ann Arbor Paperbacks, 1959
The Elegies and The Songs and Sonnets, ed. Helen Gardner, Oxford University Press, 1963
The Divine Poems, ed. Helen Gardner, Oxford University Press, 1978
Selected Prose, ed. Neil Rhodes, Penguin, 1987
John Donne: The Major Works, John Carey ed., Oxford, 1990
Selected Letters, ed. P.M.Oliver, Carcanet, 2002
The Poems of John Donne (Longman Annotated English Poets), ed. Robin Robbins, in two volumes, Longman, 2008
John Donne on Death, Foreword by Edward Docx, Hesperus, 2008

Biography
Izaak Walton, 'The Life of Dr. John Donne' (1640; rev.1658) in *Selected Writings*, ed. Jessica Martin, Fyfield Books, 1997
John Donne: A Life, R.C.Bald, Oxford, 1970
Donne: The Reformed Soul, John Stubbs, 2006

Criticism
'The Metaphysical Poets' in *Selected Essays*, T.S.Eliot, Faber & Faber, 1932; revised 1999
'Donne After Three Centuries' in *The Common Reader: Second Series*, Virginia Woolf, 1935
'The Line of Wit' in *Revaluation*, F.R. Leavis, 1936
John Donne: Life, Mind and Art, John Carey, Faber, 1981
A Preface to Donne, James Winny, Longman, 1983
John Donne: The Critical Heritage, ed. A.J.Smith and Catherine Phillips, in two volumes, 1975 & 1996

Biographical Note

Nicholas Robins works at Shakespeare's Globe. He has written for the *London Magazine* and the *TLS*, is the author of *Walking Shakespeare's London* (2004) and a co-editor of the third edition of *The Oxford Guide to Literary Britain and Ireland* (2008).

HESPERUS PRESS

Hesperus Press is committed to bringing near what is far – far both in space and time. Works written by the greatest authors, and unjustly neglected or simply little known in the English-speaking world, are made accessible through new translations and a completely fresh editorial approach. Through these classic works, the reader is introduced to the greatest writers from all times and all cultures.

For more information on Hesperus Press, please visit our website: **www.hesperuspress.com**